Investing for Beginners and Options Trading

The Ultimate Step-by-Step Crash Course to Create Passive Income from Home, with Top Strategies for Investing in Forex, Stock Market, ETFs, and Real Estate

BENJAMIN WHITE

INVESTING FOR BEGINNERS

BY

BENJAMIN WHITE

TABLE OF CONTENTS

INTRODUCTION

Investment is significant from numerous perspectives. Before investing, it is fundamental to comprehend what a venture is and its significance.

Investment is a demonstration of contributing cash to procure the benefit. It is the initial move towards the future security of your cash.

Investment: The need for it

The investment can help you later on whenever contributed carefully and appropriately. According to human instinct, we plan for a couple of days or think to get ready for the venture; however, we don't place the arrangement enthusiastically. Each individual must arrange for the venture and keep aside some measure of cash for what's to come. Most likely, what's to come is dubious, and it is required to contribute sagaciously with some specific arrangement of activities that can stay away from budgetary emergencies for the purpose of time. It can assist you in bringing a splendid and secure future. It gives you a secure future, yet besides, controls your spending design.

Significant Factors of Investments

Getting ready for Financial investment - Planning assumes an urgent job in all fields. For the money related venture, one must have a relevant arrangement by taking all ascent and fall circumstances of the market. You ought to have a decent learning of investment before making arrangements for money related ventures. Sharp perception and methodology are the essential requirements for effective monetary investment.

Contribute as indicated by your Needs and Capability-The reason behind the venture ought to be clear by which you can satisfy your needs from the investment. In venture, money related capacity is likewise a part that can bring you fulfillment and whatever outcomes you need. You can begin venture from a modest quantity according to your capacity. You should think about your salary and security to pick the best arrangement for you.

Investigate the market for accessible venture alternatives - The investment market is loaded with circumstances; you can investigate the market by applying the legitimate methodology. You can take help from money related organizers, administrators who have intensive information about interest in the market. Investigate the probability of investment markets and contact the wonderful tallness of progress by reasonable venture choices.

By taking assistance from an accomplished, capable monetary organizer and merchants can likewise give you the certainty to do well in the field of the venture. Presently the inquiry strikes the mind that what are the kinds of ventures?

Kinds of Investments

Common Funds-Basically, the shared reserve is an overseen venture support in which cash is destroyed from the financial specialists to purchase the protections.

Securities exchange

It is where different individuals exchange all-inclusive and acquire the greatest quantifiable profit. Nonetheless, it is fundamental to know the bull and bear of the securities exchange for putting resources into it. The Stock market for venture likewise incorporates the value market and clever market. You can put resources into values and clever market and get a great sum benefit by centered methodology and sharp examination of market pattern.

Bonds - It is the ideal approach to pick up enthusiasm on your chief sum. The intrigue and timeframe depend upon understanding. In this, holder loans a specific add up to the guarantor (borrower) for a fixed timeframe. As of now, you will get the enthusiasm from the borrower, and in the wake of finishing that fixed timeframe borrower will return back your cash. A long-haul device for money related ventures.

Fixed Deposits - The Fixed Deposit (FD) administration is given by different banks that offer speculators a higher pace of enthusiasm on their stores when contrasted with an ordinary investment account. Fixed stores have the development date to pick up the arrival on investment.

Land: One can likewise put resources into the land and

manage the private and business property. This is likewise a slanting method to procure a decent quantifiable profit.

There are different money related organizers, budgetary supervisors, exchanging tips suppliers who can give you various choices for interest in the market. In any case, it is fundamental to pick the choices admirably.

We support investments that are easy, charge proficient, broadened, fluid, and straightforward. Numerous financial specialists regularly keep running into inconvenience when they put resources into things that don't have these five qualities. Ventures with these five qualities have been gainful after some time, however, they commonly are not energizing. There is commonly not a "hot story that you have to follow up on now!" related to them. The monetary administration's industry, for the most part, doesn't support these kinds of investments since they produce next to no benefit from them. We are in the matter of boosting the abundance of our customers, not the budgetary administration's industry. Remember that this rundown of investment attributes isn't complete. Different components to search for in investments may incorporate appealing valuation, low relationship to your different possessions, a decent profit yield or premium pay, a tilt towards zones of the market that have created more significant yields, for example, esteem stocks, a proper hazard level for you, and so forth.

Minimal effort. We ordinarily put resources into the minimal effort, list-based assets and trade exchanged assets (ETF's). The assets we put resources to have a

10

normal cost proportion of only 30% every year. The common effectively exchanged value shared store has a normal cost proportion of 1% or more. With venture reserves, the best indicator of future relative execution is the cost proportion on the store; the lower, the better. Speculative stock investments ordinarily have yearly cost proportions of 2% in addition to 20% of any benefits earned. Some factor annuities and lasting extra security "ventures" can have yearly costs of 2% or more. By watching out for the expenses of our ventures, we can spare our customers critical measures of cash every year and assist them with accomplishing better yields after some time (all else being equivalent). With venture items, you don't show signs of improvement execution with a greater expense item; in truth, you normally deteriorate execution.

Duty Efficient.Our investments (file-based assets and ETF's) are amazingly charged proficient, and they enable the financial specialist to have some power over the planning of the assessments. These sorts of assets have low turnover (exchanging movement), which is a typical trait of duty proficient investments. We suggest keeping away from shared assets with high turnover because of their duty wastefulness. After the ongoing huge increment in the U.S. financial exchange, numerous dynamic value common assets have "imbedded" capital increases of as much as 30%-45%. And when you purchase those shared subsidizes now, you may wind up covering capital additions government expenses on those embedded increases regardless of whether you didn't possess the reserve during the expansion. ETF's commonly don't produce long and momentary capital increase disseminations at year-end, and they don't have imbedded capital additions like dynamic shared assets. Speculative stock investments are normally charged wasteful because of their exceptionally high turnover. Notwithstanding putting resources into charge effective items we additionally accomplish numerous different things to help keep our customer assessments limited, for example, charge misfortune collecting, keeping our turnover/exchanging low, placing the correct sort of interests in the correct kind of records (charge area), utilizing misfortunes to counterbalance capital increases, utilizing possessions with huge capital additions for gifting, putting resources into tax-exempt city bonds, and so on.

We like to put resources into broadened reserves since they decrease your explicit stock hazard and the general danger of your portfolio. Awful news discharged around one stock may make it drop half, which is horrendous news if that stock is 20% of your entire portfolio, yet will be scarcely seen in a store of 1,000 stock positions. We will, in general, support finances that regularly have in any event a hundred properties and frequently a few hundred possessions or more. These enhanced subsidies give you an expansive portrayal of the entire resource class you are attempting to get an introduction to while taking out the explicit stock hazard. We are not liable to put resources into the freshest Solar Energy Company Equity Fund with 10 stock situations, for instance. We don't trust in going out on a limb (for example, explicit stock hazard) that you won't get paid for in higher anticipated return.

Basic. We lean toward investments that are straightforward, straightforward, and straightforward. If you don't get it, don't put resources into it. The majority of our ventures are basic and straightforward; we know precisely what we claim. Convoluted venture items are structured for the dealer, not the purchaser, and ordinarily have high shrouded charges. Instances of confounded and non-straightforward ventures that we, for the most part, keep away from are flexible investments, private value reserves, organized items, some disaster protection "investment" items, variable annuities, privately owned business stock, new business stock or credits, and so on. Make everything as straightforward as could be allowed, however, not less complex.

We accept most financial specialists ought to have most of their portfolio put resources into things that have these five great attributes. By doing so, you will maintain a strategic distance from a lot of errors, negative astonishments, and dangers along the way. Moreover, we accept your after-assessment investment returns will probably be higher over extensive stretches of time. Obviously, few out of every odd shrewd or wise investment will have these attributes. For instance, salary delivering land property is illiquid (and regularly not differentiated) however, can be a fantastic long-haul venture whenever acquired and oversaw appropriately. Owning your very own business is illiquid and not expanded yet can be a great method to assemble riches also. We accept these five venture attributes become much progressively significant as you enter retirement, since by then, you might be increasingly centered on lessening hazard and safeguarding your riches than building it, and you may require the liquidity to spend and to bless some portion of your riches during retirement. These five incredible investment qualities can be a decent screening gadget for potential ventures and great components to consider when contributing.

CHAPTER 1

INVESTOR PERSONALITY TYPE

There are a few investigations of financial specialist types out there, so where do you start?

The CFA Institute breaks the character types into four primary gatherings: Preservers, Accumulators, Followers, and Independents. At that point, there's the notable Bailard, Biehl, and Kaiser (BB and K) five-way model, which depends on financial specialist certainty levels and their favored speculation strategy.

The Barnwell Two-Way Model* shows up superficially to be significantly more apparent, gathering financial specialists as either "uninvolved" or "dynamic." Each investigation has its benefits, albeit every one of the three could propose that an individual's sentiments towards hazard may change depending on the situation.

One critical thought when characterizing speculator character type is the equalization of the target (what you need to pick up and why) and requirements (time skyline, liquidity, and view of hazard). Likewise, are simply the assets you are contributing, your family, your business, or your customer.

A decent inquiry to pose would be, what amount does an individual's inclination towards hazard change if, for instance, you are an institutional financial specialist? Is it accurate to say that you are bound to take no chances for a superior possibility of ROI, or would your character overrule this for conceivable more significant yields yet on a higher bet?

Psychonomic Investor Profiling

The course of ordering financial specialist character types that we'll use here depends on Jonathan Myer's study. It holds that an individual's inclination towards hazard is probably not going to change, paying little mind to condition. Psychonomic financial specialist profiling instead recommends a speculator's sentiments towards risk could be shaded by how they see that specific hazard; this is notwithstanding how they feel about cash all in all, for example, regardless of whether it harms more to lose a pound than it does to increase a pound.

Speculator Personality Types

Mindful

Preservationist in speculation decisions, they have a substantial requirement for money related security and want to keep away from high hazard adventures. This kind of speculator is bound to confide in their financial information over that of an expert consultant.

They loathe losing even the scarcest measure of cash. As a result, any speculation choices require a lot of time, thought, and examination.

Passionate

This sort of speculator is bound to confide in the gut sense as opposed to doing intensive due perseverance; they put stock in karma or fortune. They contribute with their heart instead of the head, following a "hot tip" or whatever appears to be in trend.

This hopefulness and affinity to hold onto the day can be fulfilling. In any case, it can likewise prompt a hesitance to cut misfortunes on a terrible speculation choice with the expectation that things will work out inevitably.

Technical financial specialist character

Specialized speculators settle on their money related choices dependent on hard certainties and numbers.

They're screen-watchers, effectively exchanging on value variances and prepared to hurry should they recognize a pattern right off the bat. They can discover to compensate in their practice over the top perseverance and are continually searching for the edge with regards to the most recent tech advancements.

Occupied

As opposed to being occupied, think about investing. That character type lives for the buzz of the business sectors and exchanging. Continually checking the most recent value developments, they are frequently purchasing and selling dependent on the latest piece of tattle or prattle from papers and magazine stories.

But since of this profound aversion of dormancy, it can mean these financial specialists pass up a great opportunity by not waiting at a superior cost.

Easy-going

This kind of character is progressively laid back with regards to funding and speculation, in certainty, they're bound to be the one giving their assets over to an expert counselor to deal with things.

They accept there's more benefit to be found in a hard join than money related speculations. Subsequently, when they've made a venture, they're not liable to determine the status of how it's doing until they genuinely need to.

Educated

An educated speculator is one who uses data from numerous sources before settling on any monetary choices. They have a steady eye on venture advertisements just as the economy to work out what could give them a superior possibility of return.

They will cheerfully tune in to master guidance and read budgetary feelings, just conflicting with the market after careful thought of the considerable number of upsides and downsides. They have money related certainty and have faith in their options, believing that their insight and experience will convert into long haul gains.

Did you see yourself in any of the character types?

Regardless of whether any of the above sounded valid or was excessively treacherous, the most significant thing is this: Know thyself and know thy financial specialist qualities – and shortcomings.

Maybe you realize that your heart drives you when your head should, or perhaps when contributing assets in the interest of others, you're mindful of playing things excessively sheltered when you could be earning more noteworthy returns. In either case, utilizing a venture stage, you can trust, and that makes a substantial showing of due constancy, can have a significant effect on how you contribute and could improve your ROI.

Which financial specialist character best portrays you?

As indicated by the CFA Institute, there are four unique sorts of financial specialists dependent on particular conduct inclinations. The scope of these passionate and mental social predispositions assumes a job in how people contribute.

Other types include:

· Preservers

· Gatherers

· Supporters

· Independents

Preservers

Preservers are speculators who put a solid accentuation on monetary security and protecting their riches. They frequently fixate on momentary execution and misfortunes. Preservers much rather evade chance and experience issues making a move with their speculations. Furthermore, much the same as with contributing, this conduct of being conscious and careful is the way Preservers approach their work and individual lives.

Overwhelming Bias Type: Emotional, identifying with the dread of misfortunes and powerlessness to decide/make a move.

Significant Biases: Loss aversion and the state of affairs

Contributing Style: Wealth conservation first, development second

Level of Risk Tolerance: Generally lower than normal

Supporters

Supporters are financial specialists who are progressively inactive. They will, in general, pursue the lead of their companions and partners. Adherents will likewise seek the present contributing prevailing fashion. Frequently, their necessary leadership procedure doesn't include an extended haul plan. They have little enthusiasm for as well as have little inclination for contributing.

Prevailing Bias Type: Cognitive, identifying with the following the conduct

Significant Biases: Recency and surrounding

Contributing Style: Passive

Level of Risk Tolerance: Generally lower than usual however regularly thinks hazard resilience level is higher than it is

Independents

Mentality: One should say I have set aside the effort to comprehend the speculation I intend to make, regardless of whether I pass up on chances like this.

Independents are financial specialists who are diagnostic, essential scholars. They have unique thoughts regarding contributing and need to be effectively associated with the speculation procedure. They are happy to go out on a limb and adhere to a venture intend to achieve their money related objectives. Independents will, in general, be masterminds and practitioners rather than devotees and visionaries.

Overwhelming Bias Type: Cognitive, identifying with the traps of doing one's very own examination

Active Biases: Confirmation and accessibility

Contributing Style: Active

Level of Risk Tolerance: Generally better than expected yet not as high as forceful financial specialists

Gatherers

Attitude: I should act rapidly on chances to profit.

Collectors are financial specialists who are keen on amassing riches. They like to be vigorously required by changing their portfolio assignments and possessions to economic situations and may not wish to pursue an organized arrangement. Collectors are daring individuals and are firm adherents that whatever way they pick is the right one.

Predominant Bias Type: Emotional, identifying with presumptuousness and want for impact over venture process

Useful Biases: Overconfidence and figment of control

Contributing Style: Actively occupied with essential leadership

Level of Risk Tolerance: High to exceptionally high

CHAPTER 2

FOREX TRADING: A BEGINNER'S GUIDE

The forex market is the world's most significant global cash exchanging business sector, working relentlessly during the working week. Most forex exchanging is finished by experts, for example, financiers. By and substantial forex exchanging is done through a forex intermediary - however, there is nothing to stop anybody transferring monetary forms. Forex cash exchanging enables purchasers and merchants to purchase the money they require for their business and venders who have earned money to trade what they have for progressively helpful money. The world's biggest banks rule forex. As indicated by a review in The Wall Street Journal Europe, the ten most dynamic merchants who are occupied with forex exchanging represent practically 73% of exchanging volume.

Since the business sectors for monetary forms are worldwide, the volumes exchanged each day are tremendous. For the huge corporate speculators, the incredible advantages of exchanging on Forex are:

Tremendous liquidity - over $4 trillion every day, which is

$4,000,000,000. It implies there's consistently somebody prepared to exchange with you

All of the world's free monetary forms tare exchanged - this implies you may transfer the cash you need whenever

Twenty four - hour exchanging during the 5-day working week

Tasks are worldwide which imply that you can exchange with any piece of the world whenever

From the perspective of the littler broker, there are loads of advantages as well, for example:

A quickly changing business sector - that is one which is continually evolving and offering the opportunity to profit

All around created instruments for controlling danger

The capacity to go long or short - this implies you can profit either in rising or falling markets

Influence exchanging - implying that you can profit by huge volume exchanging while at the same time having a generally low capital base

Heaps of alternatives for zero-commission exchanging

How the forex Market Works

As forex is about foreign trade, all exchanges are made up of a money pair - state, for example, the Euro and the US Dollar. The essential instrument for exchanging forex is the conversion scale, which is communicated as a proportion between the estimations of the two monetary forms, for example, EUR/USD = 1.4086. This worth, which is alluded to as the 'forex rate' implies that, at that specific time, one Euro would be worth 1.4086 US Dollars. And this proportion is continuously communicated to 4 decimal spots, which indicate that you could see a forex pace of EUR/USD = 1.4086 or EUR/USD = 1.4087 yet never EUR/USD = 1.40865. So, the furthest right digit of this proportion is alluded to as a 'pip.' Thus, a change from EUR/USD = 1.4086 to EUR/USD = 1.4088 would result in a difference in 2 pips. One pip, in exchange and this manner, is the littlest unit.

With a forex rate at EUR/USD = 1.4086, a speculator buying 1000 Euros and using dollars would pay $1,408.60. The forex rate at that point shifted to EUR/USD = 1.5020; we can say that the speculator could sell their 1000 Euros for $1,502.00 and bank the $93.40 as a benefit. If this doesn't appear to be enormous, add up to you, you need to place the entirety into the setting. With a falling or rising business sector, the forex rate doesn't just change uniformly, yet sways and benefits can be taken all the time as a price wavers around a pattern.

When you're expecting the worth EUR/USD to fall, you may exchange the other route by selling Euros for Dollars and repurchasing then when the forex rate has changed to further your potential benefit.

How Risky is Forex?

Whenever you exchange on forex as in any cash

25

exchanging, you're in the matter of money hypothesis, and it is only that - theory. It implies there is some hazard associated with forex money trading as in any business; however, you may and should find a way to limit this. You can generally set a point of confinement to the drawback of any exchange, that way, to characterize the most extreme misfortune that you are set up to acknowledge whether the market conflicts with you - and it will focus on events.

The best protection against losing your shirt on the forex market is to decide to comprehend what you're doing completely. Quest the web for decent forex exchanging instructional exercise and study it in detail-a touch of proper forex training can go far!. At the point when there are bits you don't comprehend, search for decent forex exchanging gathering and pose parts and heaps of inquiries. A large number of the individuals who routinely answer your questions on this will have proper forex exchanging online journals, and this will likely offer you responses to your inquiries as well as give heaps of connects to great destinations. Be cautious; in any case, look out for forex exchanging tricks. Try not to rush to part with your cash and research anything very well before you shell out any well-deserved!

The Forex Trading Systems

While you might be directly in being wary about any forex exchanging framework that it's publicized, there are some great ones around. A large portion of them either use forex graphs and by methods for these, recognize forex exchanging signals which advise the dealer when to purchase or sell. This sign comprises of a specific change in a forex rate or a pattern, and these will have been concocted by a forex dealer who has concentrated long haul inclines in the market to distinguish substantial sign when they happen. A significant number of the frameworks will utilize forex exchanging programming, which recognizes such hedge from information inputs that are assembled naturally from market data sources. Some use mechanized forex exchanging programming, which can trigger exchanges consequently when the sign tells it to do as such. And when these sound unrealistic to you, search for online forex exchanging frameworks that will permit you to embrace some fake exchanging to test them out. So, by doing this, you can get some forex trading preparation by giving them a turn before you put genuine cash on the table.

So, How Much do you Need to Start?

Be aware that this is a bit of a 'How long is a piece of string?' question. However, there are ways to be a beginner to start. Be also aware that the minimum trading size for most trades on forex is usually 100,000 units of any currency. This volume is known as a standard "lot." Meanwhile, numerous organizations offer the office to buy in drastically littler parts than this, and a touch of web looking through will before long find these. Various adverts are citing just two or three hundred dollars to get moving! You will regularly observe the term acciones exchanging forex, and this is only a general term that covers the little person trading forex. Short scale transferring offices, for example, these are frequently called as forex smaller than usual exchanging.

Where do You Start?

The absolute most evident answer is obviously - on the web! Online forex exchanging gives you direct access to the Forex showcase, and there are parcels and bunches of organizations out there who are good to go to manage you on the web. Be cautious, do invest the energy to get some in order high forex exchanging training, again this can be given on the internet and set up your spurious record to trade before you endeavor to go live. Whenever you do well and take as much time as is needed, there's no motivation behind why you shouldn't be effective in forex exchanging along these lines, have persistence and stick at it!

As a rule, the time between the give up and opening function is short and endures just solely minutes. Benefits picked up from this role will in accepted below. Be that as it may, the all-out make bigger finished by using gigantic positions can be noteworthy. Some Forex brokers trade up to 200 conditions in a day. Indeed, no longer all posts opened by using dealers can make advantages for them, yet the decisive goal is to have a typical gain by becoming a member of all positions.

One tip is that when scalping, you should post a stop-misfortune request extremely close to the opening price of the scenario for decreasing the misfortunes when there is variance toward the market. It is regularly recommended that you utilize a stop-misfortune on your scalping exchanges. As this is one of the stepped forward Forex exchanging strategies, how about we abridge this methodology and the tips a supplier ought to consent to:

• Don't preserve a role open for too long; ideally, the most excessive keeping time ought now not to surpass five minutes.

• The size of the trade ought to be pretty huge, as the measure of picked up pips per exchange is very little.

• The higher the extent of the day by way of day exchanges is, the higher the odds are of being fruitful with Forex scalping.

• This machine is official for informal investors, implying that you would most presumably need to invest a high-quality deal of energy changing to accomplish effects with it.

Positional Trading

This is positively a progressed Forex technique, as it is utilized by way of the top-acquiring dealers. The preferred imperative function of this system is that it requires notably much less everyday consideration. In any case, it has to be completed effectively with a cautious lengthy haul show off the investigation. Most Forex changing structures are carried out on little league outlines, implying that most of them are day exchanging procedures.

Positional replacing is something no longer quite the same

as day replacing – and it's in particular not the same as scalping. At the factor when a provider starts exchanging positions, they are relied upon to preserve a scenario for a severe vast stretch. It is difficult to distinguish the base suggested keeping time as it mainly relies upon the dealer's diagram of the market, and the number of pips picked up.

When utilizing positional exchanging, one of the most progressive Forex strategies, a dealer wishes to do the whole thing in totally the contrary route contrasted with Forex scalping; the other measurement will in ordinary be relatively little in correlation with the exchanging capital. While scalping, you exercise to open sizable situations, as you are hoping to make a couple of pips for every exchange. During positional exchanging, you intend to get more than 100 pips, which can make your role higher impenetrable when the market vacillates.

Technical strategy

Technical analysis is essential when buying and selling Forex or any different asset. The fundamentals would possibly set the path of a pair, but the professional evaluation dictates the entry and exit tiers of your trades. If you pass by the technicals, you may also give up dropping even if your assessment is impeccable. So, FX Leaders continuously update its technical Forex techniques to replicate the altering market stipulations and assist you in becoming aware of exact entry and exit points, as nicely as how to manage yourself when in a trade.

Fibonacci Indicator – Forex Trading Strategies

The Fibonacci buying and selling approach is one of the most customary and, in many instances, used long-term technical techniques on the Forex. It tries to location charge motion in the desirable context by the usage of the Fibonacci sequence, a close illustration of the historical "Golden Ratio." Fibonacci numbers are no longer solely frequently used in the economic markets but are additionally utilized to physics, geometry, engineering, and art.

Regarding Forex trading, there are many makes use of this particular mathematical construct. This unique Fibonacci trading approach is dependent on a phenomenon called a "pullback." To wholly apprehend how pullbacks work, we ought to first discuss a more critical thought — the trend.

A style is genuinely a directional go in rate over a defined period. When looking at every rate alternate individually, it can be a challenge to find an excellent pattern. However, through searching at the larger picture, traits are effortlessly identifiable. Spotting a strong trend is a necessary section of imposing a Fibonacci trading strategy. Without the presence of a trend, this approach is of limited effectiveness and impact.

Breaking Down The Fibonacci Trading Strategy

The picture above demonstrates a decently short pattern, which is the sort of design that we will concentrate on when separating this specific Fibonacci exchanging methodology. The trend comprises of three legs: two going up and one going down.

Since the general bearing of the pattern is up, the center part, where there is a fleeting ruin, is known as a "pullback." The issue with recognizing pullbacks is that when we see a pattern begin to switch, it is complicated to understand a withdrawal from an inversion of the design. It is the place the Fibonacci exchanging system comes in. The method enables us to break down the information, assess value activity, and specialty an official conclusion.

Fibonacci numbers and proportions have been acclaimed among mathematicians and artisans for a long time. They are found much of the time all through nature and, when applied to the monetary markets, can work as extraordinary explanatory apparatuses. No math is required to utilize these numbers — the product exchanging stages play out every vital figure for us. By and by, executing a Fibonacci trading methodology Forex is direct and intuitive. The principal undertaking that we should finish is to settle on a choice dependent on the lines which show up on the chart.

Applying The Fibonacci Sequence

On the graph over, the Fibonacci proportions are the purple lines drawn evenly. They speak to the 38.2%, 50.0%, and 61.8% retracements of the predominant upturn. By looking at how far the pullback has come to on the Fibonacci scale, we can decide two things: regardless of whether the cost will resume to the bull or turn around into a crisp bearish pattern. In any case, we can arrange to exchange every potential situation.

The general Fibonacci exchanging methodology standard expresses that as long as the value stays over the 61.8% line, we can anticipate that the pattern should proceed. It shows the bearish value activity is just a pullback, not an out and out inversion. On the other side, when the value crosses the 61.8% line, we should regard it as the beginning of a bearish pattern. And when we are long this market, the time has come to finish off and proceed onward to the following exchange.

Investigation

The diagram above delineates a pullback that structures a base at around the half Fibonacci marker. It shows the cost will in all likelihood rise, and the general upward pattern will proceed. As per this reality, we can modify our exchange of the board appropriately. If we are long this market, at that point holding the position is legitimate exchange the executives' methodology. If we are searching for a short section, at that point, hanging tight for a better exchange area is the play.

In any case, the utilization of the Fibonacci grouping has given us a solid structure for making position the executive's views on-the-fly. We are currently ready to routinely recognize our optimal assume benefit and stop misfortune value levels. With this data, we can offset chance with remuneration and expand or compensate while restricting danger.

Even Levels – Forex Trading Strategies

Even Levels is one of the least complex yet fantastically helpful thoughts in Forex exchanging. Low levels are significant in most Forex trading techniques and help us in dissecting outlines. So, in any case, they can likewise be made use of individually as a procedure as opposed to only a device for different techniques. By viewing the most explicit value changes and drawing their low levels, we can make fruitful exchanges. In thoroughly understanding the flat degrees of increasingly complex outlines, we can spot slants that we would have generally missed.

The significance of flat levels

Most merchants believe low levels to be similarly as significant as value activity, which is the center to Forex exchanging. Dissecting the blend of the value change and the low levels can enable us to comprehend the pattern and foresee where the market will go straight away. Albeit even levels are an exceptionally fundamental Forex exchanging technique, numerous renowned and experienced dealers, for example, Jesse Livermore, Warren Buffett, and George Soros, have affirmed that they use it as a premise to a large number of their systems.

Low levels help us spot key zones on a diagram where an adjustment in the pattern is probably going to happen. This can help us when choosing where to put a stop, or when we need to enter an exchange yet don't have a clue about the correct time to do as such. Exact planning can be critical in numerous Forex exchanging techniques, and a careful investigation of the even levels can enable us to locate the right planning and spot a decent exchange. Remember that even levels might be the establishment for some techniques; however, all alone, it usually is insufficient and must be utilized in blend with other Forex exchanging methodologies.

Even Levels and 'Swing Points'

The ideal approach to utilize even levels furthering our potential benefit is by breaking down the swing focuses. Swing focuses are focuses on where the pattern changes, and by stamping even levels at these focuses, we can see costs where it is likely as an adjustment in a model. The outline beneath unmistakably indicates how we can utilize even levels to further our potential benefit.

Notice how the swing focuses tend to rehash themselves. Bolster levels can transform into obstruction levels and the other way around. By denoting the low levels on the graph, we can anticipate when the following swing point will happen and enter/leave an exchange at the ideal time. The circles on the diagram are the focuses that we ought to have had the option to see in cutting edge. These are the clearest passage focuses, and by seeing them, we would have given an edge to any methodology that we utilized.

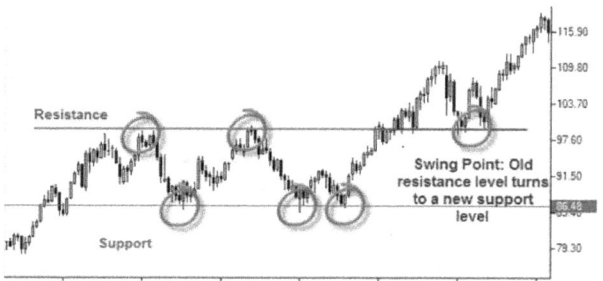

Horizontal Levels and Ranging Markets

Parallel ranges are also beneficial in range-bound markets. Range-bound markets are markets where the rate has evident upper and decrease boundaries that the charge doesn't cross. By observing the cost as it processes one of the limitations, we can predict with tremendous accuracy where the fee will fashion next. As always, the fee can be unpredictable and might smash the boundary just as we determine to enter a trade, but overall, this approach is very reliable and safe.

Head and Shoulders – Forex Trading Strategies

As we have already talked about 'Candlestick Trading Strategy', which permits us to recognize the candlestick charts and what every candlestick indicates. However, in reality, grow to be a master of the charts, we ought to study a few frequent chart patterns and what information we can draw from them about the future.

So, the 'head and shoulders' pattern is one of many recognizable and tradable chart patterns. In Forex jargon, they are acknowledged as "shampoo" due to the fact of the shampoo company of the equal name. The Head and shoulders Forex patterns consist of an excessive height in the middle and two double peaks on both facets of that one, as can be viewed in the illustration below. The higher height is the head, and the two decrease ones are the shoulders. The pattern itself appears like a head between two joints. As a result, the name.

Head And Shoulders Trading

Head and shoulders patterns emerge as applicable when the neckline is penetrated. Once the neckline is broken, we may additionally seem to be to open a brief function on the contrary aspect of the head and shoulders buying and selling indicator.

Some merchants enter immediately, while others prefer to come on a pullback and retest of the neckline. The latter alternative is safer because now we recognize that this is now not just a fake-out. The range of pips targeted in this method is identical to the wide variety of pips between the top of the head and the neckline. So, when the market is feeling right, and there is extra room to go after attaining the target, we may aim for higher earnings and let the exchange run.

Head And Shoulders Forex Pattern: A Typical Candlestick Chart

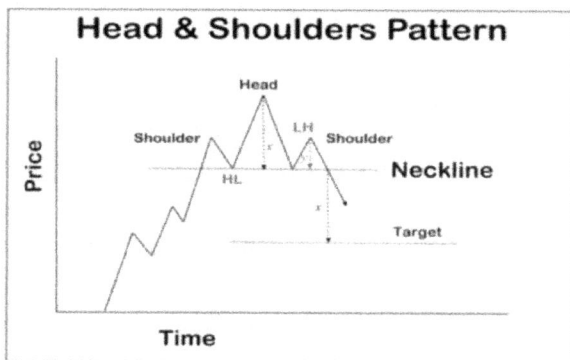

This picture above is apparent and allows for precise attention of the head and shoulders trading pattern. Don't count on the actual charts to be as clean — they will supply extra of a challenge. To change these patterns, we have to spot them in real-time as they happen, no longer after they are irrelevant.

The bottom line, usually referred to as the neckline, is a guide level. It might also now not continually be a straight line, but an ascending or descending sequence. The slope element to the neckline makes it a whole lot extra hard to spot; thus, we ought to center of attention on the larger picture. Junior traders must likely switch to a line chart, which makes some patterns extra visible, as an alternative of the candle chart. The photograph below is a real chart displaying a head and shoulders Forex pattern. Recognizing the head and shoulders trading sample in real-time and buying and selling it efficaciously is a great deal extra tricky than shown here in the illustrations.

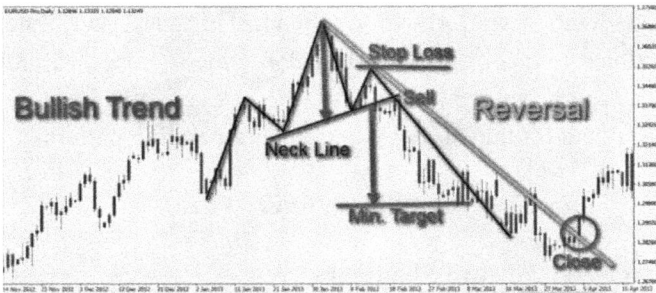

Spotting Head And Shoulders Forex Patterns

As cited above, the neckline should be damaged for the head and shoulders pattern to be usable. Nonetheless, real-life trading doesn't follow textbook guidelines so strictly. We have to be smart and flexible to spot these patterns as they are forming, to minimize the danger and maximize the profits.

One trick for early pattern cognizance and coming into high chance prevailing trades is to look at the volumes. No count number the time frame; the amount is supposed to decrease with each peak. And of course, as with most things trading, this isn't always the case. The reduced volume on the 2d height, which is the head, means that customers had an attempt on the upside, but besides a great deal force. As a result, the rate subsequently goes down.

So, when we are at the top of the 2nd shoulder and quantity is low, we need to check different symptoms such as RSI and Stochastics to see if the pair is overbought. And if that's the case, and if pins, inverted hammers are forming on the candlestick chart, then we might enter the trade with a stop above the head. This way, we almost double the income target and enlarge the risk-reward ratio. The chart beneath illustrates the use of this head and shoulders trading strategy but on an ascending pattern.

The volume Decreases With Every Peak.

Inverse Head And Shoulders

'Backwards Head and Shoulders' examples are something contrary to head and shoulders. All principles apply. However, they are topsy-turvy. For this situation, the neck area additionally fills in as obstruction. It implies we should hope to purchase upon the break of the neck area. Like head and shoulders, they might be straight, climbing, or sliding.

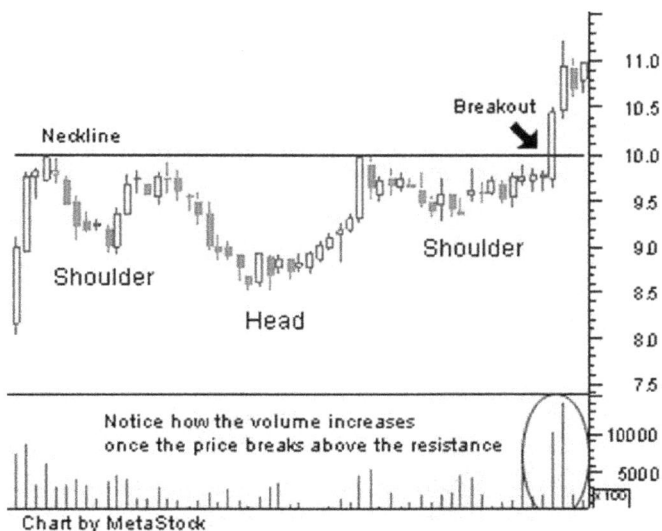

Chart by MetaStock

Opposite Head And Shoulders Trading Is Exactly The Same But Upside-Down.

Head and shoulders examples are not a Forex exchanging technique all alone. In any case, they do assist us with getting a superior picture of what is happening and what will occur straightaway. Having the option to detect these examples can be the distinction between a triumphant exchange and a losing one.

As you acquire understanding as a broker, have a go at fusing whatever number of these procedures into your exchanging system bin as could reasonably be expected. Likely outcomes are improved execution and a chance to get more cash-flow.

41

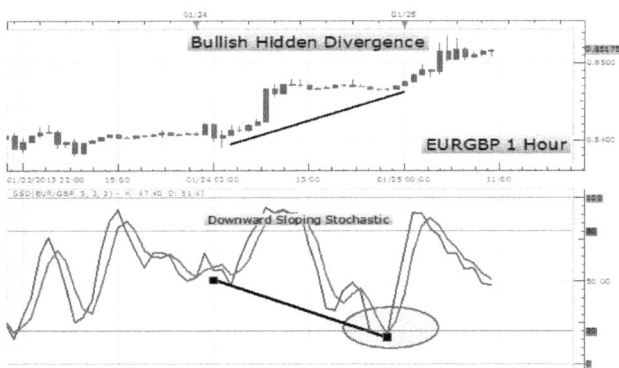

Uniqueness – Forex Trading Strategies

Besides basics, sellers and analysts of cash related instruments use different pointers to understand what may come to pass for the expense of a particular tool. These pointers offer a central system for seeing plans and envisioning what course the cost will slant.

For the most part, these pointers are what makes Forex signals possible. They consider a total steady assessment of significant worth action, and the gathering here at FX Leaders realizes them on a regular reason.

What Is Divergence?

Dissimilarity is a primary marker used by our professionals at FX Leaders to assist increase benefits. The chance of entering the market at the opportune time the correct way increments on every occasion utilized related to different pointers, for example, Moving Averages (MA), RSI, Stochastics, or distinctive assist and opposition levels.

What Is Divergence Trading?

By genuinely recognizing the title "difference," one can without an awful lot of a stretch tell that uniqueness replacing is a type exchanging mounted in disharmony or deviation. Disparity Forex exchanging methods are as frequently as feasible utilized with the aid of cash dealers around the world.

In principle, expenses and pointers have to go a similar way at equal rates. On the off danger that the value arrives at a higher high, at that factor, the marker has to arrive at a more significant high. On the off threat that the benefit comes at a decrease steep, at that factor, the pointer needs to go with the identical pattern. The equal applies to lower lows and higher lows.

In the match that the fee and the related pointers don't associate, at that point, you can tell that some progress is going to happen. The excellent markers to use in dissimilarity changing are Stochastics, RSI, MACD, and Trade Volume.

A bullish distinction occurs when the award in the marker is extra advantageous than the difference in the price — bearish disparity is a unique way. While applying this differentiation, there are four indispensable sorts of dissimilarity:

• Regular Bullish

• Hidden Bullish

• Regular Bearish

• Hidden Bearish

We will make clear every kind and how to trade the concerning disparity Forex procedure.

Regular Bullish

Standard divergences are utilized as an apparatus to exhibit inversions. This EUR/USD month to month outline demonstrates the fee of making a decrease low for two days. In any case, the energy in MACD and Stochastics didn't relate to that of the cost activity, making higher lows. This hedge a possible inversion of the sample or perchance a comply with the downtrend or something similar.

'In reverse Head and Shoulders' models are something in opposition to head and shoulders. All standards apply, anyway they are essential upside down. For this circumstance, the neck zone furthermore fills in as an obstacle. It infers we should plan to buy upon the break of the neck zone. Like head and shoulders, they may be straight, climbing, or sliding.

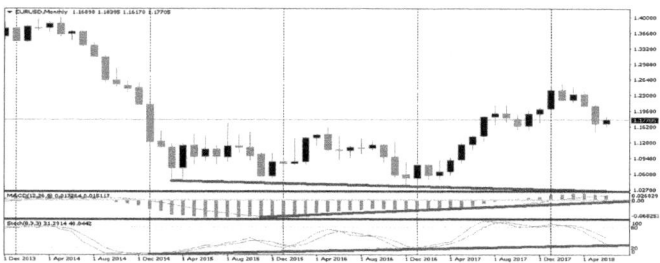

Regular Bearish

As we can see from the USD/CHF chart, the price reached a high in the previous week and then made a higher high the following week. On the other hand, the MACD indicator at the bottom of the chart is making lower highs. This is called 'Regular Bearish Divergence' and indicates a fall in the price to come.

In this case, since we are in an uptrend, we should expect a retracement. After entering at the top, we should look to get out of the trade at the uptrend line.

Regular Bearish Divergence – The price is making higher highs while MACD is making lower highs.

Unlike regular divergence, hidden divergence indicates a continuation of the trend. This EUR/USD chart shows the occasion where the price was making higher lows, while the stochastic was making lower lows. This divergence indicates that the retrace down is over, and trend continuation is about to resume.

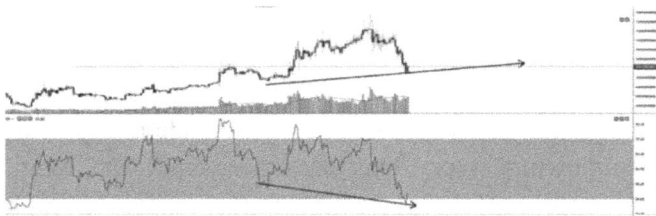

Hidden Bullish Divergence – unlike regular divergence, hidden divergence indicates the continuation of the trend.

Hidden Bearish

The daily EUR/USD chart below gives a clear example of hidden divergence and the trend reversal that follows. We can see that when stochastic was nearing overbought levels and had established separation with the price, which made lower highs, the pair fell immediately and began a downtrend. This sort of chart pattern means that when the stochastic was overbought the second time, EUR/USD buyers couldn't push any higher. So, the upside was complete even though EUR/USD couldn't make new highs. This is a bearish reversing signal.

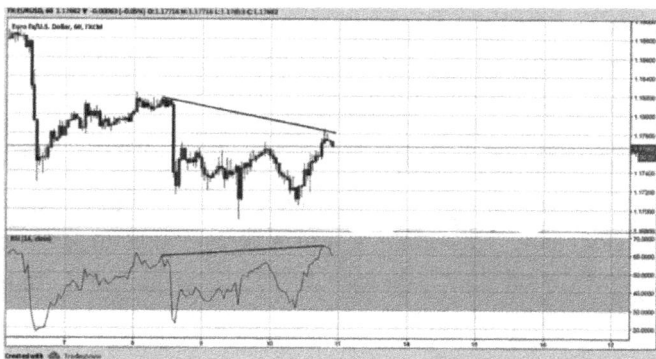

Hidden Bearish Divergence – when Stochastics are nearing overbought levels, the pair falls immediately to continue the downtrend.

When Using Divergence Forex Strategies

Divergence is quite easy to spot, as it only requires drawing a few lines. Nonetheless, sometimes we look too hard at the charts. This makes us see things that aren't there.

During periods of consolidation or low liquidity, small divergences between price and indicators might form — but that doesn't mean we should consider them real discrepancies. The chart below shows a four-day consolidation period with symbols, and the price does not correlate accurately. However, this setup does not constitute a divergence.

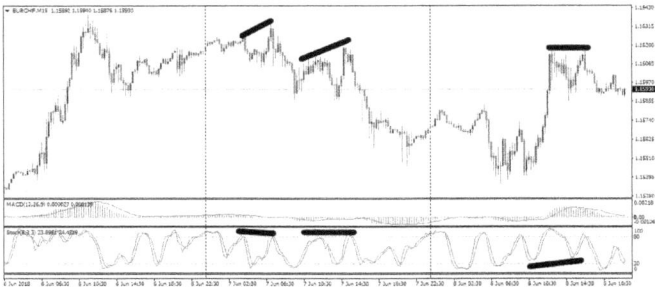

In union periods, not everything that resembles difference is dissimilarity — be cautious.

Dissimilarity is probably an ideal approach to utilize pointers to examine diagrams. Close by other help and obstruction techniques, the uniqueness Forex exchanging can be used to give your diagnostic aptitudes the push they have to make you a genuinely gainful broker. And when you need to discover how disparity exchanging is utilized in live market circumstances, investigate our week after week examination from April 17-23. In our week by week investigation, our top Forex specialists clarify how they use uniqueness exchanging, close by other Forex systems to dissect the market's activities consistently.

Candle Strategy in Forex

Neither one of the candlesticks examples can be an exchanging signal itself, nor would it be able to be utilized for a showing of the potential sections. The model demonstrates the desires in the market and signalizes the possible changes. For looking for the passage, another technique for examination, as opposed to candles, ought to be utilized.

If you lean toward day exchanging, being doubtful to pointers, at that point Japanese candle Forex exchanging system would live up to your desires. Candle examples empower a broker to decide the market circumstance just as organic market balance.

Characteristics of the candle design investigation

The more extended the «body» of the candle in Forex, the more grounded the Momentum and the more prominent the possibility to move in the indicated bearing. A bullish candle with the enormous body and the short shade demonstrates that the purchasers impact the market more than the dealers. A «bearish» flame with the colossal body and quick «shade» implies that the market supply is more grounded than interest. A long «shade» explicit way suggests that during the time spent the candle's arrangement in Forex; the organic market parity has moved. The progressions of the market desires can be dictated by contrasting the candles and one another.

The little shade from either side demonstrates more prominent odds of the development distinct way. Generally equivalent «shades» gave the candle's body is little (Doji candles for Forex design) speaks to advertise uncertainty - the weight on the purchaser's and dealer's cost is around the equivalent. In such conditions, even a little development in volume of exchange may cause a stable value development; all the more regularly, there is a pattern to switch.

The principle candle exchanging frameworks:

The candle designs which might be characterized as inversion examples caution about inversion pattern as well as about the parallel development start or exit from it; and now and then about decrease of the development's speed without altering of the course. Any example bodes well just where it arrives at the most grounded level. If an inversion example succeeds, at that point, it will be trailed by constant distinct development.

All exchanging examples made up of 1-2 candles would lose their importance if, during current development (pattern or revision in value development), this example applied more than once. This is particularly valid for Doji candle designs. The most dependable Japanese candle sign shows up on the Daily period. Following time allotment decline, the unwavering quality of the sign brings down.

A case of exchanging candles technique dependent on Engulfing design

Candle Forex exchanging system utilizes this candle design as an inversion signal or the revision starts.

Trading asset: It is any currency pair.

Trading period: This is the European and sessions.

Timeframe: This usually D1 or H1.

Candlestick trading strategy for a signal to buy:

The development of a candle «engulfing» example is required on the low of the descending pattern.

The sign is affirmed: it tends to be a Doji candle example or one all the more Engulfing case a similar way.

Low of the first Engulfing example must not be recharged; in addition - the more remote the value, the more grounded an exchanging signal.

Right now of the following candle opening, we will open a long position. Stop Loss will be fixed underneath a Low affirmation sign.

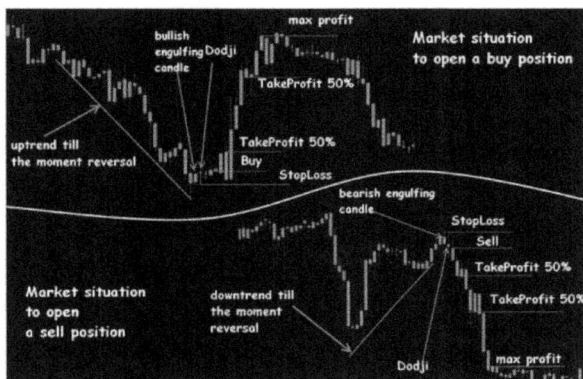

Candlestick strategy Forex for the signal to sell:

The development of the candle «engulfing» example is required on the high of the upward pattern.

The sign is affirmed: Doji candle example or one all the more Engulfing case a similar way.

High of the first Engulfing example must not be recharged.

We will open a short position right now of the following candle arrangement. Stop Loss will be set over the High affirmation signal.

The candle Forex methodology with «Free candle» pointer

The exchanging methodology utilizes candle designs with a high unwavering quality level and sliding standard for the assurance of the present pattern. EMA(9) is prompted for the famous money pair exchanging on the M15 period.

«Free candle» is viewed as a full-fledged 15-minute flame, body, and shade of which don't contact the EMA (9) line, and the end cost of the candles in Forex exchanging isn't higher/bring down the past outrageous. «Free candle» must have the typical «body» and regular «shade» («hammer,» «dodgy» inversion examples, and GAP are not relevant).

I am exchanging resources: EUR/USD, USD/JPY, USD/CHF, GBP/USD, EUR/GBP, EUR/JPY, GBP/JPY.

I am exchanging period: the European and the US exchanging session. Candle Forex exchanging the times of the market's uncertainty isn't fitting.

The fundamental pattern's heading is dictated by EMA(9). For the extended position (purchase), the presence of the «free» bullish flame above EMA(9) is required. The rear light's entrance after «free candle» or a Buy Stop request ought to be somewhat higher than the end cost. The Stop Loss is fixed at the maximum level of the free candle.

And for a short position (sell), a «free bearish candle» ought to be fixed underneath the moving normal. The section at the opening of the following flame relies upon the market or ought to be made by a pending Sell Stop request. A Stop Loss ought to be fixed 3-5 beneath min of the «free light.

For the setting of Taking Profit, two scopes of the free light ought to be used.

A decent minute for the section with regards to candle

system exchanging respect to first cash sets shows up inside 15-30 minutes after the European session opening when the market bearing has been resolved. The standard length of the open arrangement is as long as 60 minutes. It isn't prescribed to exchange without Stop Loss or enter inside initial 5 minutes of every hour.

The arrangement ought to be opened except if:

good ways from shutting cost of the «free candle» to EMA(9) is under 3-4;

The body of the «free candle» is under 10.

From the scientific desire planned, the «free candle» Forex candle exchanging is adequately viable, if the arrangements are not made time after time and just in dependable designs.

Ascending Triangle Pattern

This triangle example has its upper side level and the lower one climbing. As such, the highest points of this triangle are on a similar level, and the bottoms are expanding. This sort of triangle regularly has a bullish character. When you recognize this triangle on the outline, you ought to be set up to catch a bullish value move equivalent to in any event the size of the triangle. As such, breakouts through the upper level (the level side) is utilized for setting section focuses for long positions. This is a sketch of the rising triangle outline design:

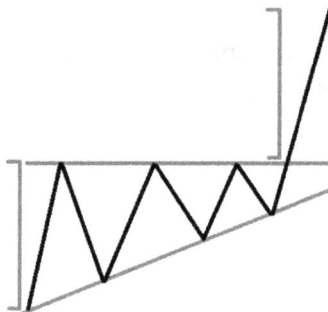

The dark lines above show the value activity inside the triangle development. The blue lines allude to the sides of the triangle, which contains the value activity. The red lines relate to the size of the triangle and its potential objective, which is commonly a 1:1 estimated move. At the point when an ascending triangle is framed during a bullish pattern, we anticipate a continuation of the design.

Diving Triangle Pattern

As noted before, the climbing and slipping triangles are an equal representation of one another. In that capacity, the sliding triangle example has the contrary trademark. The flat side of the sliding triangle is underneath the value activity. The upper side of the triangle is slanted downwards. In a bearish market, the plunging triangle has a bearish potential equivalent to in any event the size of the example. Thus, the sliding triangle is utilized to open short positions after the cost has broken its lower (level) side. How about we see the sketch of the slipping triangle:

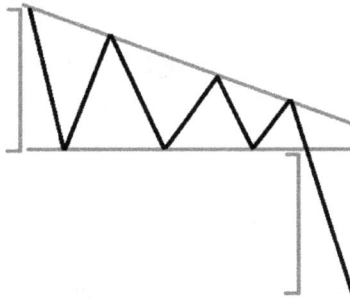

At the point when the dropping triangle is made during a bearish value propensity, we anticipate that the pattern should proceed.

It is essential to refer to that the rising and the plunging triangles some of the time get through the slanted level, causing false hedge and catching a few merchants en route. Similar remains constant at the level cost zone. You ought to consistently attempt to sit tight for the end of the flame to affirm the breakout. This will help lessen a significant number of the bogus sign.

Rising/Falling Wedge

The rising and falling wedges are like the mounting and the sliding triangle designs. Notwithstanding, the rising and the falling wedges have no flat side. The two sides of the prongs are inclining a similar way. We should portray the two sorts of wedges you will discover on the value outline.

Rising Wedge

This is a triangle diagram design, where the two sides are slanted upwards. The value makes higher tops and considerably higher bottoms. This makes the two rising lines collaborate, creating a kind of triangle design on the diagram. The rising wedge has a solid bearish character. As such, the trigger side of the wedge example is the lower line. When you recognize a breakout through the lower level of a rising wedge, you ought to expect a sharp value drop equivalent to at any rate the size of the example. In this manner, breakouts through the lower level of a wedge are utilized for opening short positions. It is what the rising wedge arrangement resembles:

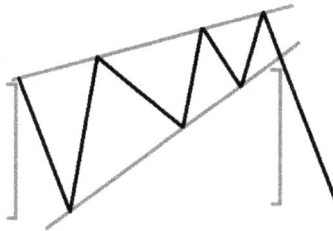

Falling Wedge

With the falling wedge design, the two sides are slanted downwards. The value makes lower bottoms and even lower tops. This way, the different sides of the triangle are sliding and agreement to a sharp point. Inverse to the rising wedge, the falling wedge has a solid bullish character. In this way, the trigger side of the falling wedge arrangement is the upper line. At the point when the value breaks the top degree of a falling wedge, you should go for a bullish move at any rate as tremendous as your wedge arrangement. Brokers utilize the falling wedge to set a long section that focuses on the graph. Underneath you will see a sketch of a falling wedge:

Since you recognize what the rising and the falling wedges appear as though we should share one more insight into these developments. Wedges could have pattern continuation, or pattern inversion character. At the point when the wedge shows up after an all-encompassing value move, we anticipate an inversion of the pattern, when the wedge shows up prior in the design, we expect that it should be an impermanent retracement that will proceed with the principle model set up. Ordinarily, the more dominant wedge development is the potential pattern inversion arrangement, which happens after a delayed pattern move.

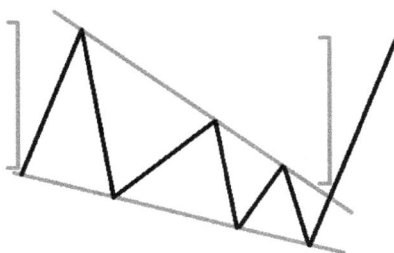

Symmetrical Triangle Pattern

The even triangle is a circumstance on the graph where the highest points of the value activity are lower, and the bottoms are higher. Additionally, the different sides of the triangle are slanted with a similar point. This makes the balanced character of the triangle.

Ordinarily, with balanced triangle design, the normal directional breakout is obscure. The purpose behind this is bullish, and the bearish move has equivalent quality as observed through the value activity.

At the point when a breakout in the end happens, it is probably going to incite a value move equivalent to the size of the example. In this manner, you ought to deliberately distinguish a potential breakout in the upper and the lower level of the balanced triangle to take the exact situation in the market. The sketch underneath shows the equitable triangle development and conceivable breakout situations:

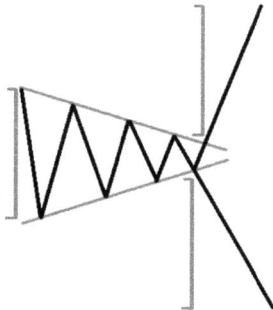

As you see from the model over, the potential objective

depends on the size of the triangle development. With this kind of estimated move investigation, you will realize what's in store from the balanced triangle breakout, regardless of whether it breaks upwards, or downwards.

Hedges

Hedges on the diagram have a comparable shape to that of even triangles. They normally show up during patterns and have a pattern continuation character.

Bullish Pennant

The bullish pennant is like a balanced triangle in appearance, yet the Bullish hedge arrangement comes after a cost increment. Since hedges have pattern continuation character, the bullish hedge is probably going to proceed with the bullish pattern on the graph. At the point when the upper side of the hedge gets broken upwards, we are probably going to see an expansion equivalent to at any rate the size of the hedge, and normally bigger.

Thus when exchanging hedges, a subsequent objective ought to likewise be utilized to get a more significant move. When figuring the following goal, you would break down the value leg promptly following the hedge. You could set the objective to 1:1 of the past leg or .618 of that leg. At the point when the pattern appears to be stable and has a lofty slant, a 1:1 estimated move would be a suitable second target, and in every other case, the .618 of the leg could be utilized. How about we investigate the bullish hedge underneath:

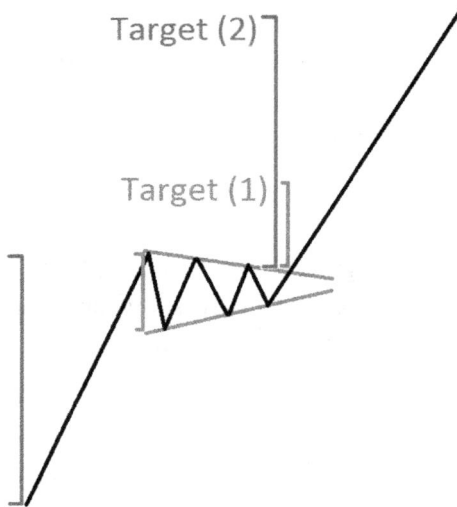

See that here we have two targets. The red objective is the first, which is as large as the size of the fence. The green goal compares to the size of the past up move, which ought to be applied beginning from the upper side of the hedge.

Bearish Pennant

As you have most likely speculated, the bearish hedge is the equal representation of the bullish fence. Bearish hedges start with a value decline and end up with a balanced triangle appearance. Since hedges have pattern proceeding with character, bearish hedges are probably going to proceed with the bearish pattern.

At the point when the cost experiences the lower level of the bearish hedge, you should initially hope to catch the main objective, which is equivalent to the size of the fence itself. At the point when the value finishes this objective, you would then be able to attempt to get the further normal diminishing, which is equivalent to the size of the past leg or .618 of that leg. Allude to the picture underneath for a Bearish Pennant:

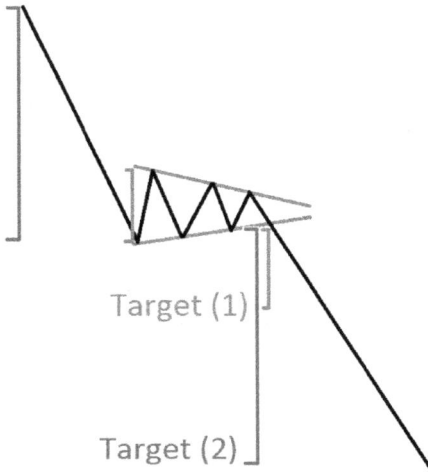

Target (1)

Target (2)

Expanding Triangle

You can scarcely ruin an extending triangle on the outline. The explanation behind this is it has one of a kind parameters. The two sides of the extending triangle are slanted, however, in inverse headings.

The course of the potential value move of this outline example is precarious to decide. In this way, we will currently present a couple of standards, which will assist you in identifying the heading of the average value moves.

Symmetrical Lines

And when the growing triangle is a flat, perfect representation of a balanced triangle, at that point, you should exchange the arrangement as a pattern continuation design. The picture beneath demonstrates a sketch of a growing triangle with stable lines:

Increasing Lines

If the different sides of the ever-increasing triangle are expanding, at that point, the example is probably going to have bearish characters.

Decreasing Lines

If the different sides of the extending triangle arrangement are diminishing, at that point, the figure is probably going to have bullish potentials.

One Side Stronger than the Other One

If the highest points of the cost activity are expanding, yet the bottoms are diminishing with a higher force, at that point, the example has bearish character. Despite what might be expected, if the bases are decreasing, yet the tops are expanding with a higher force, at that point, the example is probably going to have bullish character. As it were, you should exchange the heading of the side, which has a higher tendency.

Trading: Triangles in Forex

Since we have examined the greater part of the significant triangle designs in Forex, I will presently demonstrate to you how a triangle exchanging framework could function.

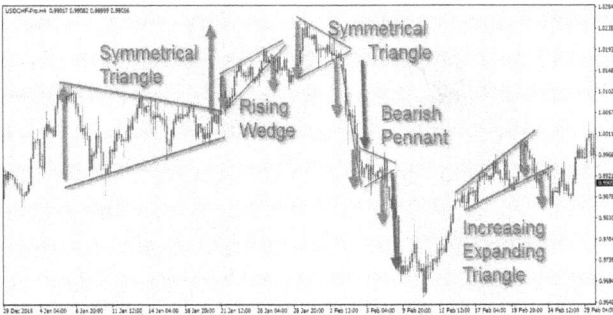

The picture above demonstrates the H4 diagram of the USD/CHF Forex pair for Jan – Feb 2016. The graph shows five triangle models and their likely results.

The diagram begins with a significant even triangle. The cost makes three diminishing tops and three expanding bottoms on the graph. The red bolt toward the start of the triangle estimates its size. As you see, a similar red flash is applied when the value breaks the upper degree of the triangle. The red glow demonstrates the potential objective of the example, which gets finished the following seven days.

Then, in transit up the value activity makes a rising wedge graph design. As we talked about, the rising wedge has bearish potential. With the breakout through the lower level of the wedge, we see a minor amendment. (yellow bolts)

Toward the finish of the bullish inclination, the value makes another balanced triangle. Later on, the amount gets through the lower level and finishes the size of the example (pink bolts).

While diminishing, the value activity makes a bearish hedge. This is the union after the primary motivation of the bearish pattern. The value breaks the lower level of the hedge subsequently. In transit down, we see the value finishing the main objective, which equivalents the size of the fence (red bolts). At that point, the lessening proceeds, and the decline is stretched out to a size equivalent to the last leg. (green pins).

The USD/CHF then makes a twofold base inversion example and changes to a bullish course. In transit up the value, activity makes a growing triangle design. Notice that both the lower and the upper level of the example are expanding. For this situation, the average value move is bearish and ought to be equivalent to the size of the case. Meanwhile, this time, the size of the matter is estimated from the closure side of the arrangement. The explanation behind this is we take the broadest side when we measure the standard move from the triangle breakout. The red bolts on the outline demonstrate to us that this example likewise finishes its objective.

Triangles are among the most significant diagram designs in Forex exchanging.

You have a contracting triangle on the outline when the tops and the bottoms of the value activity are pushing toward one another.

The basic Forex triangles involve:

· Climbing Triangle: level tops, higher bottoms, bullish potential.

· Plummeting Triangle – level bottoms; lower lids; bearish potential;

· Wedges – sides increment/decline in a similar heading;

· Rising Wedge – higher tops; much higher bottoms; bearish potential;

· Falling Wedge – lower depths; even lower lids; bullish potential;

· Balanced Triangle – lower tops; higher bottoms; sides have a similar edge of development

· Bullish Pennant – comes after cost increment; closes with a little balanced triangle; bullish potential

· Bearish Pennant – comes after abatement; fastens with a bit of even triangle; bearish potential;

· Growing Triangle – sides move against one another. The capability of the growing triangle fluctuates relying upon the tendency of the line:

· Sides are Symmetrical – the potential value move is toward the pattern.

· The two Sides are Increasing – bearish likely

· The two Sides are Decreasing – bullish potential

CHAPTER 3

SWING TRADING BASICS: MEANING AND HOW IT WORKS

The way toward swing exchanging has turned into a well-known stock trading technique utilized by numerous dealers over the market. This style of exchanging has demonstrated to be exceptionally useful for some dedicated stocks and Forex dealers. Customarily swing exchanging has been characterized as a progressively theoretical methodology as the positions are generally purchased and held for the dealers foreordained time allotment. These time allotments could run somewhere in the range of two days to a couple of months. The objective of the swing broker is to distinguish the pattern either up or down and place their exchanges in the most invaluable position. From that point, the merchant will ride the design to what they decide as to the depletion point and sell for a benefit. Intermittently swing brokers will use a wide range of specialized markers that will enable them to have a progressively good likelihood when making their exchanges. Shorter-term brokers don't really will in general swing exchange as they lean toward holding positions for the day and practicing them preceding the end of the market. The swing exchanging technique uses time, and it is the time the impediment factor for long-time dealers. Generally, there is a lot of hazards associated with the end of the market and that a merchant won't acknowledge this hazard.

Swing exchanging is a style of exchanging that endeavors to catch increases a stock (or any monetary instrument) over a time of a couple of days to a little while. Swing brokers principally utilize specialized investigation to search for exchanging openings. These brokers may use principal examination, notwithstanding breaking down value patterns and examples.

Swing exchanging is a more extended term transferring style that expects persistence to hold your exchanges for a few days one after another. It is perfect for the individuals who can't screen their outlines for the day; however, they can devote two or three hours examining the market each night.

This is likely most appropriate for the individuals who have all day employments or school yet have enough extra time to keep awake-to-date with what is happening in the worldwide economies.

Swing exchanging endeavors to recognize "swings" inside a medium-term pattern and enter just when there is by all accounts a high likelihood of winning.

For instance, in an upturn, you intend to purchase (go long) at "swing lows." And on the other hand, sell (go short) at "swing highs" to exploit transitory countertrends.

Since exchanges last any longer than one day, more

significant-stop misfortunes are to climate instability, and a forex merchant must adjust that to their cash the board plan.

You will, in all likelihood, observe exchanges conflict with you during the holding time since there can be numerous variances of the value during the shorter periods.

Significantly, you can try to avoid panicking during these occasions and trust in your examination.

Since exchanges more often than not have more significant targets, spreads won't have as quite a bit of an effect on your general benefits.

Thus, exchanging sets with bigger spreads, and lower liquidity is worthy.

You should be a swing dealer if:

You wouldn't fret holding your exchanges for a few days.

You are eager to take fewer exchanges; however, progressively cautious to ensure your transactions are generally excellent arrangements.

You wouldn't fret having enormous stop misfortunes.

You are understanding.

You can resist the urge to panic when exchanges move against you.

You might NOT have any desire to be a swing dealer if:

You like quick-paced, activity stuffed exchanging.

You are fretful and like to know whether you are correct or wrong right away.

You get sweat-soaked and on edge when exchanges conflict with you.

You can't put in two or three hours consistently to break down the business sectors.

You can't surrender your World of Warcraft striking sessions.

The differentiation of swing exchanging is an expansive point in that it has various impacts from a massive number of different exchanging procedures. These exchanging procedures are exciting and have their particular hazard profiles. Swing trading can be an excellent path for a market member to improve their specialized investigation abilities further while allowing them a chance to give more consideration to the leading site of the exchange. Numerous fruitful swing brokers have been known to utilize a Bollinger band procedure as an apparatus to help them in entering and leaving positions. For a swing dealer to be useful at the methodology, they should have a high bent for deciding the present market pattern and putting their situations as per that pattern. It makes a swing dealer note high to put a short position with the arrangement of holding for an all-inclusive timeframe in a market that is slanting upwards. The general subject here is that the objective of the dealers ought to be to build their likelihood of progress while restricting or wiping out hazard-totally. The swing dealer's most noticeably awful foe is that of a sideways or in a dynamic market. Sideways value activity will stop a swing merchant cold in their tracks as there is no overall pattern to key off.

At the point when utilized forcefully swing exchanging is a superb system used by numerous merchants crosswise over different markets. It isn't just in the Forex showcase; however, it is a critical apparatus in fates and value markets. Swing dealers take the abilities that they learn through specialized examination and can even parlay these aptitudes into different alternative techniques. The transient idea of swing exchanging separates it from that of the conventional speculator. Speculators will, in general, have a more extended term time skyline are not influenced by momentary value variances. As usual, one must recollect that swing exchanging is just a single technique and ought to be used only when adequately comprehended. Like any exchanging system, swing trading can be unsafe, and preservationist methodologies can transform into day exchanging procedures rapidly. When you utilize a swing exchanging system, guarantee that you completely comprehend the dangers and build up a technique that will have the option to enable you to produce the most significant rate returns on your positions.

Swing exchanging is one of transferring styles which generally executed in theoretical action in monetary markets, for example, securities, item, foreign trade, stock, and stock record. Usually, this exchanging style requires a swing dealer to hold their exchanging position more than one exchanging day, generally 2 to 5 exchanging days. Swing trading is mainstream in exchanging world as this transferring style, for the most part, has a decent hazard and reward proportion, it implies the likelihood to pick up benefit is higher than the risk that may ascend in each exchange.

By and large, swing exchanging goes for 100 pips benefit likelihood. Benefit potential can be picked up from each market swing. A swing broker, particularly in foreign trade and stock file advertise, can go both long or short of accepting each open door. It likewise implies, inside an exchanging week, when a market is unpredictable, a swing dealer may run over a few exchanging openings the individual in question can take.

Contrasted with scalping exchanging or day exchanging, clearly swing trading has less trading chances, notwithstanding, as should be visible here and whenever you execute this exchanging style, most likely you will have more opportunity to do your different exercises as you don't need to keep your eyes on a market all the exchanging day. You will get fewer chances, however, with a high likelihood of winning for every opportunity. It is your call to pick which exchanging style to apply. No exchanging style is immaculate, and there is always in addition to and short.

Presently, and when you surely need to give an attempt to swing exchanging, you can discover a few procedures from numerous assets accessible on the web. You may find a few books and some other instructive materials on swing exchanging. You can visit and be an individual from some exchanging discussions too. Notwithstanding, as regular, I need to advise you that there are likewise some shifty individuals guaranteeing themselves as swing exchanging masters; however, they need you to purchase their refuse training materials. Be mindful of such individuals.

Luckily, in the wake of getting some essential comprehension and experience on swing exchanging, you can be a decent swing merchant also. You can even think of your swing trading systems. Numerous individuals appreciate the advantage of building up their swing trading systems as they are the main ones who realize their exchanging character, need, and style. Never quit to figure out how to be a decent swing merchant, even though unquestionably, it will require some investment to ace swing exchanging brilliantly yet, at last, the majority of your endeavors will payout.

Issues With Swing Trading Using Options

Swing exchanging is one of the most widely recognized methods for trading the securities exchange. Regardless of whether you know it or not, you presumably have been swing exchanging all these while. Swing trading is purchasing every so often selling a couple of days or weeks after the fact when costs are higher, or lower (on account of a short). Such a cost increment or lessening is known as a "Value Swing," subsequently the expression

"Swing Trading."

Most learners to choices exchanging take up opportunities as a type of influence for their swing exchanging. They need to purchase call choices when costs are low and afterward rapidly sell them a couple of days or weeks after the fact for a utilized addition. The other way around valid for put choices. In any case, many such amateurs immediately discovered the most painful way possible that in options swing exchanging, and they could, in any case, make a generous misfortune regardless of whether the stock inevitably moved toward the path that they anticipated.

How is that so? What are a few issues related to swing exchanging utilizing alternatives that they neglected to observe?

For sure, although choices can be utilized just as utilized substitution for exchanging the underlying stock, there are a couple of things about alternatives that most tenderfoots neglect to observe.

1) Strike Price

It doesn't take long for anybody to understand that there are numerous alternatives accessible crosswise over many strike costs for every single optionable stock. The undeniable decision that fledglings generally make is to purchase the "modest" out of the cash alternatives for more significant influence. Out of the cash, choices are alternatives that have no work in an incentive in them. These are called options with strike costs higher than the overarching stock cost or put choices with strike costs lower than the overall stock cost.

The issue with purchasing out of the cash alternatives in swing exchanging is that regardless of whether the essential stock move toward your expectation (upwards for purchasing call choices and downwards for purchasing put choices), you could at present lose ALL your cash if the stock didn't surpass the strike cost of the options you bought! The truth is out; this is known as to "Lapse Out Of The Money" which makes every one of the choices you purchased useless. This is likewise how most fledglings lose all their cash in choices exchanging.

By and large, the more out of the cash the choices are, the higher the influence, and the higher the hazard that those alternatives will terminate useless, losing all of you the capital put into them. The more in cash the choices are, the lower increasingly costly they are because of the worth incorporated with them; the lower the influence turns out to be, nevertheless, the more economical the danger of terminating useless. You have to take the average extent of the move and the measure of hazard you can mull over when choosing which strike cost to purchase for swing exchanging with choices. And when you anticipate a significant move, out of the cash choices would give you immense rewards, yet if the movie neglects to surpass the strike cost of those choices by termination, a terrible arousing is standing by.

2) Expiration Date

Not at all like swing exchanging with stocks which you

can clutch never-ending when things turn out badly, have alternatives of a distinct lapse date. It means that you are incorrect; you will rapidly lose cash when lapse lands without the advantage of having the option to clutch the position and hang tight for arrival or profit.

Indeed, swing exchanging with choices is battling against time. The quicker the stock moves, the surer you are of benefit. The uplifting news is, all optional stocks have options crosswise over numerous termination months too. Closer month options are less expensive, and further month alternatives are progressively costly. All things considered, when you are sure that the hidden stock is going to hurry, you could exchange with closer termination month alternatives or what we call "Front Month Options," which are less expensive and subsequently have a more significant influence.

Exchange forex and CFDs on stock files, products, stocks, metals, and energies are with an authorized and controlled representative. For all customers who open their first genuine record, XM offers up to $5000 store reward to test the XM items and administrations with no underlying store required. Study how you can exchange more than 1000 instruments on the XM MT4 and MT5 stages from your PC and Mac, or an assortment of cell phones.

The amount Money Do I Need to Swing Trade Stocks?

Keen on swing exchanging stocks–taking exchanges that last a couple of days to half a month and thinking about what amount of cash you have to begin? How much capital you'll need is reliant on the procedure you use, which at that point influences the amount you chance per exchange and your position size.

Markets You Can Swing Trade

Swing exchanging is taking a place that could take the most recent days to half a month (possibly several months for individual brokers/exchanges). To what extent a swing exchange keeps going relies upon the procedure you're utilizing and what you anticipate from your trades. And when a stock moves typically 1% every day, and it needs to move 10% so as to arrive at your objective (where you need to get out with a benefit), it could take half a month or more before the value advances toward your leave point (if current conditions proceed).

Swing brokers hold positions medium-term, in contrast to informal investors (perceive How Much Money Do I Need to Become a Day Trader?) who close all situations before the day closes. Procedures shift by swing dealer. However, the first spotlight is on force swing merchants need to catch a conventional piece of value development in the most limited measure of time conceivable. At the point when the value energy closes, swing brokers proceed onward to different chances.

This style of exchanging should be possible in many markets (stocks, forex, fates and choices, for instance), which have the development you can benefit from (profit!). Swing exchanging stocks is well known because there's continuously a stock moving with force someplace.

Forex is likewise mainstream because, for the most part,

there's a money pair (or a few) that are moving admirably. Prospects are also exceptionally mainstream among day and swing merchants, offering a full cluster of items (for example, gold, bonds, stock records, instability, espresso, and so forth) to exchange. Swing exchanging forex requires less capital than stock and is hence a decent choice And when you need more cash-flow to swing exchange stocks.

Take a look at specific situations in the financial exchange, so you can perceive how a lot of cash you'll have to turn into a securities exchange swing merchant.

Issue of Under-Capitalization When Swing Trading Stocks

Having more capital in your record is superior to less. One primary slip-up dealers are under-promoted. In the stock, advertise being under-promoted can without much of a stretch occur particularly to new brokers if their record drops in worth.

As showed, to make it worth our time and energy, we ought to change in any event $100 per exchange. Along these lines, our victors won't be disintegrated by commissions and expenses. Be that as it may, And when we hazard $100, what occurs if a dealer's record parity drops to $4,000? Presently they are gambling 2.5% on each exchange. If things still don't go well, and the equality drops to $3,000, the broker is currently risking 3.3% per trade they are risking more as their presentation deteriorates!

If your record parity dips under $5,000, STOP TRADING, since you can never again bear to lose $100 and still keep the record hazard to under 2%. Likewise, And when you opened a record with $15,000, and you said you would hazard 1% exchange, if your parity falls beneath $10,000, quit exchanging. And when you continue trading with an equalization beneath $10,000, you will hazard over 1% (gambling at any rate $100 per exchange).

Top up your record to bring it back above $5,000 (or $10,000 if gambling 1%) And whenever you are as yet particular about your technique (or are eager to place in an opportunity to make it work), or just pick not to exchange until you are in a superior situation to do as such.

Cash Needed to Swing Trade Stocks – Final Word

The snappiest method to perceive how a lot of capital you need is to utilize the pursued equation:

Exchange chance x position size x (100%/account hazard %) = Capital Required.

Expect your chance 1% of your record, purchase 100 offers, and your exchange hazard is $2 (purchase at $38 and stop misfortune at $36). Module the numbers:

$2 x 100 x 100 = $20,000. That is the amount you have to make that exchange. You could use influence (up to 2:1), which implies that you need $10K in the record to make this because with influence, you will have the required $20K. You will need to have more in the record than the definite sum you need!

In case you're willing to chance 2% of your record per exchange:

$2 x 100 x 50 = $10,000 capital required.

Record hazards and exchange hazards help you decide how much capital you will require. Each exchange is somewhat unique, with various exchange dangers and position sizes. Record for that when determining the amount you will store. Concentrate the stock graphs, choose how and where you will enter and where you will put a stop misfortune.

When in doubt, you will require at any rate $5,000 to $10,000 to swing exchange stocks successfully. It is prescribed you store more than the base, supposing that you save the absolute minimum a couple losing exchanges will put you beneath the suggestion record balance.

It's smarter to hold up a couple of months and set aside more capital than to surge in under-promoted and likely lose everything. Utilize an opportunity to rehearse while you set aside!

Swing Trading - How to Trade?

Key learning:

It sounds incredible when you consider swing stock exchange; however, the majority of the brokers are unconscious of the technique on the best way to exchange. In swing, transferring the merchant by and large revels into buying the stocks toward the path where the pattern is stable. In straightforward words, the swing merchant will never exchange the course, which isn't in the stream and not coordinating up the design. These exchanges are hung on for a couple of days, and as a rule, they monitor the higher time allotment outlines, which are around 1 hour and more than that while you are observing and setting your exchanges.

There are a few recognized manners by which a swing dealer can without much of a stretch spot his/her exchanges and that additionally toward the prevalent pattern. The standard and effective practice are to sit tight at the cost level to remake previously, and you have to enter your exchange before it reaches out towards on stream. The passage is done for the most part based on value resounding off of help or opposition levels, pattern lines, or by and large it might require marker check.

In swing stock exchanging, the swing financial specialists or brokers can without much of a stretch have the chances heaped in their benefit by watching the more prominent and more significant period graphs and by entering the exchanges just the method for meaningful patterns in the securities exchange. These will make your business an incredible style of exchanging regardless of the securities exchange.

Figure out How to Swing Trade: In request to figure out how to swing exchange, you have to have the authority over the central segments of the exchanging. Every one of the subtleties that are talked about underneath structures the structure hinders the swing stock trading and are the reasons why outrageous expert financial specialists are incredibly beneficial.

This territory grasps the accompanying:

o **Trading brain science -**

You have to create adjusted Psychology to wind up fit for exchanging effectively.

o **The money, the executives -**

This administration allows a merchant to limit the dangers and to expand the arrival esteem on their rewards.

o **Market investigation -**

In the assessment, there are two different ways, which are Technical and essential investigation.

o **Japanese candle graphs -**

It is the main component to have an inside investigation of the financial exchange and its feelings. You should be for perusing and understanding the Japanese candle arrangements.

o **Trend Identification -**

The swing brokers increment their chances by exchanging the course of the pattern. You have to discover the right design.

o **Support and opposition levels -**

These two levels grant the merchant to locate the pivotal degrees of the securities exchange where the patterns are in the dealer's support.

o Fibonacci retracement levels -

Much the same as the help and obstruction levels, the Fibonacci retracement levels additionally enable you to have a decent passage into the market.

o Trading markers -

The apprentices must take a gander at the pointers, which are commonly utilized by the banks and expert financial specialists in swing exchanging.

o Stop misfortune -

Stop misfortunes bring about only a little harm; accordingly, it's disregarded by the majority of the newcomers around here.

o Trading hours -

Continuously cause a decent search and after that to find your hours that are appropriate for the opening and shutting of the trades.

Swing Trading: Swing Trading Stock That Help You Earn More

The term alludes to the different styles of swing exchanging stock, items, or list. This exchanging is an exchanging practice where the merchant purchases or sells the instrument at or close to the finish of a down or up value swing in the ware. This swing is caused either because of day by day value unpredictability or week by week value instability. Information on these styles encourages him to become a beneficial dealer and puts him on the way of effectual exchanging calling.

The time furthest reaches that is typically associated with holding the instrument by the merchant is 1-4 days. It is, for the most part, not precisely seven days, regardless. The money or the swing is exchanging stock, which the merchant is managing in swings starting with one value level then onto the next. A swing broker rides on this wavering or swing that the market makes on the stock. That implies he purchases the instruments toward market patterns, and he doesn't exchange by conflicting with the significant trends in the market.

There are various manners by which he can put an exchange. The most well-known method for doing it toward market pattern is to sit tight at the costs swing, exchanging stock to return or backtrack and afterward enter an exchange before it goes onwards. It is the most secure technique as he can stack the chances in support of him by watching the higher period graphs, and after that enters the exchange, the bearing of significant pattern likewise got back to the draw time. There are some essential components of swing exchanging that should be aced to turn into a capable dealer.

The above all else component in learning the swing exchanging business is a comprehension of the exchanging brain research. The other significant viewpoint requires knowledge of the meaningful patterns of the market. It causes him to distinguish the model effectively in the market and increase from it. The third considerable viewpoint is the dealer's capacity to oversee cash with the goal that he container expand gains and limit dangers. The dealer ought to likewise have the option to peruse and comprehend the Japanese Candlestick development to get a vibe of the market opinions. Another component that is urgent to his prosperity is to have the option to discover the best exchanging hours to open and close the exchange.

Different fundamentals of a decent merchant are to find what pointers are utilized by other expert dealers to run swing exchanging effectively. He should likewise be knowledgeable about the Trading markers used by different banks. He ought to also have the option to distinguish the specialized market investigation and the essential market examination as the two most significant styles to break down the market. Among another component of the swing exchanging business is the information of help and obstruction levels, Fibonacci retracement level, stop misfortune, and recognizable proof of pattern lines.

The dealer needs to acclimate himself with this data to begin his voyage to turning into an effective swing broker.

Swing Trading Stocks - An Insight to Pros and Cons

There are sure contrasts between Swing Trading Stocks and Day Trading. Day Trading is identified with a specific timeframe, though Swing exchanging likewise delineates a specific timeframe. Swing exchanging includes a timespan that is longer than the staring off into space-time range and shorter than somebody who is headed to contribute and exchange for a more extended timeframe. If there should be an occurrence of records and assessment purposes, whatever is not exactly a year is imagined as a transient exchanging the financial exchange, and anything that is about a multi-year or more is considered as long haul evaluating.

Swing exchanging is a novel style of exchanging and venture. It is reasonable for each one of the individuals who need to exchange for a more extended timeframe than a day trading and have a decent learning of swing transferring procedures. The informal investors enter and exit around the same time and in a similar position. The swing merchants would leave their exchange of stocks and items to be open for a couple of weeks, which can stretch out as long as a couple of months. The merchants work as indicated by the swing exchanging methodologies they know.

Swing Trading Stocks Pros and Cons:

Like all other things, Swing exchanging has its high side and awful side. Bothe the day trading and swing trading are similarly dangerous, which relies upon the experience, specialized assessment and brain science as upheld by the merchant. Continuously recollect the standard that is, the more drawn out the time of exchange the market, the higher the hazard factor.

The Pros of Swing Trading Stocks-

*It is less tedious than the day exchanging segment.

*A dealer possesses more energy for the assessment of the best-exchanging methods between the exchanges, and like this, the broker can most likely choose great and fascinating entertainers.

*The first section which is reduced is offered time to get recuperated from the harm and afterward go to a positive level or state-contingent upon the bearing the merchant has chosen. It is said that a long position that is upward posts are substantially more superior to the principal short area that is descending location.

*Swing Traders doesn't require to address the issues of the 'Example Day Trader.'

*Swing merchants are permitted to have more information for concentrate as indicated by the period than the informal investors.

*A swing broker is progressively sure and certain about his/her exchange because the ongoing pattern of exchanging is bolstered by the long haul information from the history.

The Cons of Swing Trading Stocks-

*Definitely the swing trader consumes less time and possesses more energy for the assessment of the best-exchanging methods between the exchanges and accordingly, the dealer can likely choose great and fascinating entertainers.

The con: is that a swing merchant may get awful information and subtleties into the information assessment and might choose a less valuable stock execution or lost stock or item.

*The first passage which is weak is offered time to get recuperated from the harm and after that go to a positive level or state-contingent upon the heading, the broker has chosen. It is suggested that a long position that is upward posts are substantially more superior to the primary short area that is descending location.

The Con: the main miserable and awful section has the opportunity to get going the other way to the trade.

CHAPTER 4

STOCK MARKET:

Newbie financial exchange speculators are the individuals who have moderately simple learning and involvement in the contributing circle. The more significant part of these people, for the most part, start by adhering to a 'purchase and hold' exchanging methodology. As a tenderfoot, your extensive involvement in financial exchange ventures in trading. Generally, it limits you to making close to a few exchanges maybe on a month to month premise from a money account. In any case, this doesn't essential connote that you have not set high requirements on your financial exchange exchanging exercises. You, in all likelihood, are keen on extending your insight just as speculation involvement in understanding the goals you may have set. It is all pleasant and great.

As a rule, it is continuously extreme for youngsters to observe timberland from just trees. Additionally, they think that it's difficult to perceive if the future possibilities of a specific security are favorable, regardless of whether the momentary exchanging patterns are not unpredictable. Apprentices are regularly competent during robust 'buyer' markets. Be that as it may, shockingly get themselves confused on harder events, mainly when market unpredictability is higher, and 'bears' happen to run the show. Ithe event that you profoundly feel you fit this depiction to the T, here then are some financial exchange venture nuts and bolts for learners, which could be helpful.

Mistakes you should consider

#1 Not Understanding the Investment in question

One of the world's best financial specialists, Warren Buffett, alerts against putting resources into organizations you don't get it. This implies you try not to purchase stock in organizations when you don't comprehend the plans of action.

#2 Falling in Love With a Company in particular

Time after time, when we see an organization we've put resources into progress nicely, it's anything but difficult to experience passionate feelings for it and overlook that we purchased the stock as a venture.

#3 Lack of Patience

How often has the intensity of gradual advancement turned out to be unavoidably clear? Gradual more often than not beats the competition - be it at the exercise center, in school, or your vocation. Why, at that point, do we anticipate that it should be unique about contributing? A moderate, consistent, and taught approach would go significantly further as time goes on than going for the latest possible time.

#4 Too Much Investment Turnover

Turnover, or hopping all through positions, is another arrival executioner. Except if you're an institutional financial specialist with the advantage of low commission rates, the exchange expenses can destroy you - also the momentary assessment rates and the open door cost of passing up the long haul increases of wise speculations.

It is crucial for you to completely comprehend that all individuals have to change degrees of hazard resilience. It surely implies there is nothing of the sort as 'right equalization' in this given issue.

It typically prompts a diminishing of the general nervousness you will undoubtedly encounter when you exchange or put resources into the securities exchange, due to your 'view' of the dangers in question. In this way, by setting aside the vital effort to completely comprehend your accurate hazard resistance, you will have the option to abstain from exchanging ventures you fear. In a perfect world, you ought not to put resources into an advantage, which can cause you restless evenings. Tension triggers dread that, in its turn, prompts a passionate reaction to the stressor. By continually holding a calm mind during securities exchange vulnerability, you will have the option to cling to an 'apathetic' necessary leadership process in your financial exchange exercises.

Make it a propensity to keep off your feelings from your ventures.

By a wide margin, the most significant obstruction a

seriously huge number of amateurs need to face routinely is their failure to direct their feelings and continue to settle on sensible choices. For the time being, the costs of organization stocks relate to the consolidated feelings of the entire venture network. At the point when most securities exchange financial specialists happen to be on edge about a specific firm, it's stock costs will undoubtedly dive in. On the other hand, when most dealers have a positive point of view to a firm, it's stock costs will generally rise.

Those people who hold a pessimistic point of view about the securities exchange are known as 'bears.' While those that have inspirational standpoints to the equivalent are known as 'bulls.' During market hours, the persistent battle among bulls and bears thought about the continually fluctuating protections' costs. These transient changes by and large emerge from bits of gossip, hypotheses, and at times even expectation. These components can be marked as being feelings. A successful financial exchange venture requires a legitimate and efficient investigation of an organization's benefits, the board, and future possibilities.

Managing all these puzzling considerations can trigger a great deal of stress, especially and when you always screen the costs of the protections you exchange. This feeling can, in the end, brief, you take certain activities. As your feelings are the primary inspiration, it is for the most part, and likely your business will not be right. At the point when you purchase a stock, you should do as such for legitimate reasons. Likewise, you ought to have practical desires for precisely how the costs will perform if your controlling rights demonstrate to be exact. At long last, before putting resources into any stock, consistently set aside an effort to decide the definite point you will sell your property, particularly if your reasons are refuted. With everything taken into account, always have a suitable 'leave' system before buying any stock, and make it a point to execute it apathetically.

Make it your business to extensively find out about the nuts and bolts of financial exchange speculation.

Preceding making your absolute first financial exchange venture or exchange, ensure that you see entirely every one of the nuts and bolts of the economic transaction together with the individual protections which make them up. The following are the absolute most appropriate zones you will be obliged to be well familiar with before starting any securities exchange exercises.

Make it a point to expand your securities exchange ventures.

The minute you have played out all the vital research that encourages you to decide and even measure chance, settling on the choice to differentiate your financial exchange portfolio can be an extremely wise advance. The equivalent is additionally the situation when you are absolutely 'agreeable' that you will have the option to pinpoint any potential threat, which may gently imperil your case. In the two locations, you will have the opportunity to sell your securities exchange speculations preceding continuing any risky misfortune.

The essential main thrust which persuades them to do so is the firm assurance that a separate ominous occasion can never impact every one of their property. What this truly comes down to is the evident certainty that stock expansion can permit to quickly recuperate from the departure of a solitary and even a few of your speculations.

The most common errors not to commit

Securities exchange contributing is a dangerous game, specific if you are an unpracticed financial specialist. And when you are not cautious, you can undoubtedly observe your capital dissolve rapidly.

1. Putting resources into little top organizations.

I have been purchasing and selling shares for quite a long while now. However, regardless, it astounds me that such vast numbers of novice financial specialists toss the majority of their money into little top organizations searching for the following five-bagger or ten-bagger. They will peruse different securities exchange gatherings. They will be urged to become tied up with these modest organizations that are tipped to be the following enormous thing, yet a large portion of them will, at last, come up short, so it's mostly only betting.

A much-improved methodology is to adhere to the reliably productive huge top organizations at first, and ideally, those that have a long record of conveying development in both income and profits. At that point, you are experienced, you could then begin pondering enhancing your portfolio to incorporate a little level of little top organizations also if you so wish. There's nothing amiss with having a couple of high-chance interests in your wallet as long as the remainder of your collection comprises of increasingly secure ventures.

2. Having an uneven portfolio.

This pursues on from the last point in that you should never overextend yourself far. At the end of the day, you ought to never put all your cash into only a couple of organizations, and you should attempt to put your money crosswise over organizations in various areas if you can to spread your hazard. Inability to do so may leave you overexposed, and it could disastrously affect your portfolio if the area you are put resources into, or the bunch of organizations you are put resources into, goes down.

3. Putting resources into shares without utilizing a stop misfortune.

One of the most widely recognized errors made by unpracticed financial specialists is that they tenaciously won't utilize a stop misfortune. Presently there might be contention for saying that you needn't bother with a stop misfortune and when you are contributing Warren Buffet-style with a ten or multi-year standpoint; however, as a rule, you should adhere to a stop misfortune to contain your troubles.

See Northern Rock or any of the other UK banks, for example. If you had put resources into these organizations a year or two back, you would have seen your ventures decreased to virtually nothing. Yet, And when you had utilized a stop loss of state 10% or 20%, at that point, you would have been consequently halted out quite a while prior, and the more significant part of your capital would now be flawless.

The primary most normal slip-up I see financial specialists make is purchasing stocks basically because they are modest. There is nothing of the sort as a small stock dependent on the value alone. And when a stock cost is 50 dollars, and it controls one thousand dollars worth of advantages, then that is a great arrangement, however, it isn't as great of a method if another stock was 100 dollars and the 100 dollar stock controlled 10 thousand dollars in resources. The model could never occur, all things considered; however, the fact of the matter is essentially asking yourself what amount genuine worth am I purchasing when I put resources into this organization?

The following most significant errors speculators make is relating an organization to individual reasoning and issues that are not founded on monetary sense and expectation by any stretch of the imagination. Some of the time, individuals put resources into organizations basically because they like the organization by and by. Nothing could be an awful thought than to put resources into an organization dependent on the sheer actuality that you by and by like it. Other individuals could like the organization you want, and the organization, the executives, might be ghastly. A few people additionally contribute dependent on senseless diagram examples and volume, which infrequently work when they are utilized, putting resources into the securities exchange. Warren Buffet and numerous different renowned speculators have expressed that seeing graph examples and volume prompts disarray and seldom benefit. The facts confirm that a few brokers have made cash off specialized diagram designs, yet what a number of them reliably profit, and what the name of wealthy transient dealers do you know?

If we can work around all the mental impedances that keep us down when we purchase organizations, we CAN profit for a more secure, more joyful future over the long haul. It's every one of them a fundamental matter of purchasing all-around run great organizations, and after that clutching them for their future monetary worth

The speculation scene can be compelling and regularly advancing. In any case, the individuals who set aside the effort to comprehend the essential standards and the diverse resource classes remain to pick up altogether as time goes on. The initial step: figuring out how to recognize various kinds of ventures and what rung each involves on the "hazard stepping stool."

Nugget

Contributing can be an overwhelming possibility for apprentices, with a massive assortment of potential advantages for add to a portfolio.

The venture 'hazard stepping stool' recognizes resource classes dependent on their relative peril, with money being the most steady and elective speculations regularly being the most unstable.

Staying with list assets or trade exchanged finances that mirror the market is frequently the best way for another financial specialist.

Understanding the Investment 'Hazard Ladder'

Here are the significant resource classes, in a rising request of hazard, on the venture hazard stepping stool.

Money

A money bank store is the least difficult, most effectively reasonable venture resource—and the most secure. In addition to the fact that it gives financial specialists exact information about the premium, they'll acquire. However, it additionally ensures they'll recover their capital. On the drawback, the premium earned from money stored in a bank account only here and there beats expansion. Declarations of Deposit (CDs) are profoundly fluid instruments, fundamentally the same as money that are instruments that usually give higher loan fees than those in bank accounts. Be that as it may, cash is bolted up for a while, and there are potential early withdrawal punishments included.

Bonds

A bond is an obligation instrument speaking to an advance made by a speculator to a borrower. A run of the mill security will include either a partnership or an administration organization, where the borrower will give a fixed financing cost to the moneylender in return for utilizing their capital. Bonds are typical in associations that utilization them to back tasks, buys, or different undertakings.

The loan costs dictate security rates. Because of this, they are exchanged during times of quantitative facilitating or when the Federal Reserve—or other national banks—raise financing costs.

Stocks

Portions of stock let financial specialists take an interest in the organization's prosperity utilizing increments in the stock's cost and through profits. Investors have a case on the organization's benefits in case of liquidation (that is, the organization failing); however, they don't possess the advantages. Holders of regular stock appreciate casting ballot rights at investors' gatherings. Holders of favored stock don't have casting ballot rights yet get inclination over ordinary investors as far as the profit installments.

Common Funds

A natural reserve is a kind of speculation where more than one speculator pools their cash together to buy protections. Shared assets are not detached, as they are overseen by portfolio directors who designate and circulate the pooled venture into stocks, bonds, and different protections. People may put resources into shared assets for as little as $1,000/share, giving them a chance to differentiate into upwards of 100 individual stocks contained inside a given portfolio.

Shared assets are, in some cases, intended to emulate hidden lists, for example, the S&P 500 or DOW Industrial Index. There are likewise numerous common supports that are seen, which means they are refreshed by portfolio directors who cautiously track and modify their assignments inside the reserve. Nonetheless, these assets, by and large, have more prominent costs, for example, yearly administration expenses and front-end charges— which can cut into a financial specialist's profits.

Shared assets are esteemed toward the finish of the exchanging day, and all purchase and sale exchanges are in like manner executed after the market closes.

Exchange-Traded Funds (ETFs)

Exchange-Traded Funds (ETFs) have turned out to be very prevalent since their presentation back in the mid-1990s. ETFs are like common assets. However, they exchange for the day on a stock trade. Along these lines, they reflect the purchase and-sell conduct of stocks. This likewise implies their worth can change radically over an exchanging day.

ETFs can follow a hidden file, for example, the S&P 500 or some other "bushel" of stocks the backer of the ETF needs to underline a particular ETF with. It can incorporate anything from developing markets, items, singular business areas, for example, biotechnology or agribusiness, and the sky is the limit from there. Because of the simplicity of exchanging and broad inclusion, ETFs are well known for financial specialists.

The most common errors not to commit in ETFs

1. Being Late

Maybe the most significant slip-up with supporting is that most races to do it sometime later. That is, speculators, scramble to ensure their portfolios directly after their positions have begun to cause soak misfortunes. When a market pullback has started, you can hope to pay a higher premium for security in the choices advertise, which is the place many will go to.

2. Not Hedging for the Right Exposure

Another typical oversight with regards to supporting with ETFs is identified with financial specialists not building a particular enough arrangement, mainly on account of securing against occasion hazard. One slip-up to maintain a strategic distance from is jumbling your exposures.

For instance, if you need to fence your value portfolio comprising fundamentally of little tops, make sure to choose the proper instrument; for example, picking a backward Russell 2000 ETF over an S&P 500 one.

The other absence of particularity is increasingly quantitative.

3. Over-Hedging

There is plenty of proof that supports long haul contributing. So in case, you're a long haul financial specialist, attempting to shield your portfolio from each adjustment or occasion hazard is a surefire approach to pay a high premium for the protection you never indeed plan to utilize. Put another way, and you may accomplish more damage to your portfolio if you attempt to effectively ensure it as opposed to leaving it be (make a point to expand and rebalance).

Understandable and necessary, you most likely don't have to support for occasion hazard except if you wish to be exceptionally strategic.

Elective Investments

There is an immense universe of elective speculations, including the accompanying parts:

Land. Financial specialists can secure areas by legitimately purchasing a business or private property. On the other hand, they can partake in land speculation trusts (REITs). REITs act like common assets wherein a gathering of speculators pool their cash together to buy properties. They exchange like stocks on a similar trade.

Flexible investments and private value reserves. Flexible investments, which may put resources into a range of benefits intended to convey past market returns, called "alpha." However, execution isn't ensured, and mutual funds can see fantastic moves in yields, here and there failing to meet expectations the market by a noteworthy edge. Commonly just accessible to authorize financial specialists, these vehicles regularly require high introductory speculations of $1 at least million. They likewise will, in general, force total assets prerequisites.

Both venture types may tie up a financial specialist's cash for significant timespans.

Products. Items allude to substantial assets, for example, gold, silver, raw petroleum, just as rural items.

The most effective method to Invest Sensibly, Suitably and Simply

Numerous veteran speculators expand their portfolios utilizing the benefit classes recorded above, with the blend mirroring their resilience for hazard. An excellent recommendation to financial specialists is, to begin with, essential ventures, at that point, gradually extend their portfolios. In particular, shared assets or ETF's trade exchanged assets are a decent initial step before proceeding onward to individual stocks, land, and other elective ventures.

In any case, the vast majority are too occupied to even think about worrying about observing their portfolios every day. In this manner, staying with list subsidizes that mirror the market is a practical arrangement. Steven Goldberg, ahead at the firm Tweddell Goldberg Investment Management and long-term shared finances writer at Kiplinger.com, further contends that most people need three list reserves: one covering the U.S. value advertise, another with global benefits and the third following a bond file.

CHAPTER 5

OPTIONS TRADING:

What are the options?

An option is an agreement that permits (yet doesn't require) a financial specialist to purchase or sell a hidden instrument like a security, ETF, or even list at a foreordained cost over a specific timeframe. Buying and selling options are done on the alternatives advertise, which exchanges agreements dependent on protections. Purchasing an alternative that enables you to buy shares sometime in the future is known as a "call options," though buying an option that allows you to sell shares sometime in the not too distant future is known as a "put options."

Nonetheless, options are not a similar thing as stocks since they don't speak to proprietorship in an organization. What's more, even though fates use contracts simply as options do, alternatives viewed as a lower hazard because of the way that you can pull back (or leave) An option contract anytime. The cost of the options (it's premium) is, therefore, a level of the hidden resource or security.

When purchasing or selling alternatives, the speculator or merchant has the option to practice those options anytime up until the lapse date - so essentially buying or selling an opportunity doesn't mean you need to practice it at the purchase/sell point. In light of this framework, alternatives viewed as subsidiary protections - which means their cost gotten from something different (for this situation, from the estimation of advantages like the market, protections, or other hidden instruments). Hence, alternatives viewed as less unsafe than stocks (whenever utilized effectively).

Be that as it may, for what reason would financial specialist use options? Purchasing options are fundamentally wagering on stocks to go up, down, or to support an exchanging Position the market.

The cost at which you consent to purchase the underlying security using the options is known as the "strike cost," and the charge you pay for buying that alternative agreement is known as the "superior." When deciding the strike value, you are wagering that the benefit (regularly a stock) will go up or down in cost. The amount you are paying for that wagered is superior, which is a level of the estimation of that advantage.

There are two various types of options - call and put options - which give the speculator the right (however not commitment) to sell or purchase protections.

Call Options

A call option is an agreement that gives the financial specialist the privilege to purchase a specific measure of offers (regularly 100 for every transaction) of a particular security or item at a predefined cost over a particular test of time. For instance, call options would enable a dealer to purchase a specific action of portions of either stock, bonds, or even different instruments like ETFs or lists at a later time (by the termination of the agreement).

In case you're purchasing a call option, it implies you need the stock (or other security) to go up in cost with the goal that you can make a benefit off of your agreement by practicing your entitlement to purchase those stocks (and usually quickly offer them to capitalize on the advantage).

The expense you are paying to purchase the call options is known as the top-notch (it's the expense of buying the agreement which will enable you to in the end buy the stock or security). In this sense, the premium of the call alternative is similar to an upfront installment like you would put on a house or vehicle. When buying a call, alternatively, you concur with the dealer on a strike cost. You are given the option to purchase the security at a foreordained value (which doesn't change until the agreement terminates).

Be that as it may, for what reason would a financial specialist use alternatives? Purchasing options are fundamentally wagering on stocks to go up, down, or to support an exchanging position in the market.

The cost at which you consent to purchase the fundamental security utilizing the alternative is known as the "strike cost," and the expense you pay for purchasing that options agreement is known as the "superior." When deciding the strike value, you are wagering that the advantage (ordinarily a stock) will go up or down in cost.

The amount you are paying for that wagered is top-notch, which is a level of the estimation of that benefit.

There are two various types of options - call and put alternatives - which give the financial specialist the right (yet not commitment) to sell or purchase protections.

Thus, call alternatives are additionally a lot of same protection - you are paying for an agreement that terminates at a set time yet enables you to buy a security (like a stock) at a foreordained value (which won't go up regardless of whether the cost of the inventory available does). In any case, you should reestablish your options (commonly on week after week, month to month, or quarterly premise). Thus, alternatives are continually encountering what's called time rot - which means their worth decompositions after some time.

For call options, the lower the strike value, the more inherent worth the call alternative has.

Put Options

On the other hand, a put alternative is an agreement that gives the speculator the privilege to sell a specific measure of offers (once more, regularly 100 for each transaction) of a particular security or ware at a predefined cost over a particular standard of time. Much the same as call options, a put option permits the broker the right (however not commitment) to sell a security by the agreement's termination date.

Much the same as call options, the cost at which you

consent to sell the stock is known as the strike cost, and the premium is the expense you are paying for the put alternative.

Put options work likewise to calls, except you need the security to drop in cost if you are purchasing taken care of alternative to make a benefit (or sell the put options and when you figure the price will go up).

On the in spite of call options, with put alternatives, the higher the strike value, the more intrinsic worth the put options have.

Long versus Short Options

Not at all like different protections like fates contracts, are alternatives exchanging commonly a "long" - which means you are purchasing the options with the expectations of the value going up (in which case you would buy call options). In any case, regardless of whether you purchase put options (appropriate to sell the security), you are as yet purchasing extended options.

Shorting an option is selling that alternative. However, the benefits of the deal are constrained to the premium of the opportunities - and, the hazard is boundless.

For both call and put options, the additional time left on the agreement, the higher the premiums will be.

It is frequently that a few people discover the Option's idea hard to see; however, they have just tailed it in their different exchanges, for example, vehicle protection or home loans. In this part, it is impudent to know the absolute most significant parts of Options exchanging before we get down to the universe of alternatives trading.

Options terminologies

Strike Price

The Strike Price is the cost at which the underlying stocks can be purchased or sold according to the agreement. In options exchanging, the Strike Price for a Call Option demonstrates the value at which the Stock can be bought (at the very latest its lapse) and for Put Options exchanging it alludes to the cost at which the dealer can practice its entitlement to sell the hidden stocks (before its termination)

Premium

Since the Options themselves don't have an essential worth, the Options premium is the value that you need to pay to buy an option. The bonus is controlled by different components, including the hidden stock value, unpredictability in the market, and the days until the Option's termination. In alternatives exchanging, picking the premium is one of the most significant segments.

Fundamental Asset

In alternatives exchanging, the essential resource can be stocks, fates, records, item, or money. The cost of Options gotten from its structural support. The Option of capital gives the privilege to purchase or sell the stock at a particular cost and date to the holder — subsequently, it is about the hidden resource or stocks with regards to Stock in Options Trading.

Lapse Date

In options exchanging, every investment opportunity has a termination date. The termination date is additionally the keep going date on which the Options holder can practice the privilege to purchase or sell the Options that are in holding. In Options Trading, the termination of Options can shift from weeks to months to year's contingent available and the guidelines.

Alternatives Style

There are two significant sorts of Options that are drilled in the vast majority of the alternatives exchanging markets.

(ITM, OTM and ATM)

It is essential to comprehend the Options before you start exchanging Stock Options. A lot of alternatives exchanging methodologies are played around the option.

It essentially characterizes the connection between the strike cost of an option and the present value of the underlying Stocks. We will analyze each term in detail beneath.

Purchasing, Selling Calls/Puts

There are four things you can do with alternatives:

1. Purchase calls
2. Sell calls
3. Purchase puts
4. Sell puts

Purchasing stock gives you an extended position. Purchasing call options give you a potential long view in the hidden share. Short-selling a stock gives you a short look. Selling a bare or revealed call gives you a possible short position in the underlying stock.

Purchasing a put alternative gives you a potential short position in the underlying stock. Selling a stripped, or unmarried, but gives you a possible long place in the hidden inventory. Keeping these four situations straight is significant.

Individuals who purchase options are called holders, and the individuals who sell options are called authors of options. Here is the important qualification among holders and authors:

1. Call holders and put holders (purchasers) are not committed to purchase or sell. They have the decision to practice their privileges. This restricts the danger of purchasers of alternatives to just the premium spent.

2. Call scholars and put authors (venders), in any case, are committed to purchase or sell if the alternative lapses in-the-cash (more on that underneath). This implies a

111

merchant might be required to follow through on a guarantee to buy or sell. It additionally suggests that alternative dealers have an introduction to additional, and sometimes, boundless, dangers. This implies essayists can lose considerably more than the cost of the alternatives premium.

Theory

The theory is a bet on future value bearing. An examiner may think the cost of a stock will go up, maybe dependent on crucial examination or specialized investigation. An examiner may purchase the stock or buy a call alternative on the stock. Estimating with a call option—rather than buying the inventory inside and out—is alluring to specific dealers since options give influence. Out-of-the-cash call options may just cost a couple of dollars or even pennies contrasted with the maximum of a $100 stock.

Supporting

Alternatives were indeed concocted for supporting purposes. Supporting with other options is intended to decrease the chance at a sensible expense. Here, we can consider utilizing choices like a protection arrangement. Similarly, as you safeguard your home or vehicle, options can be used to protect your ventures against a downturn.

Envision that you need to purchase innovation stocks. Be that as it may, you likewise need to restrict misfortunes. By utilizing put options, you could limit your drawback chance and appreciate all the upside in a financially savvy way. For short dealers, call options can be used to confine misfortunes assuming incorrectly—particularly during a slight crush.

What is Options Trading?

At the point when the vast majority consider speculation, they consider purchasing stocks on the financial exchange, and many are presumably totally ignorant of terms like options exchanging. Buying shares and clutching them with the end goal of making long haul additions is one of the more typical venture systems. It's likewise a consummately reasonable to way contribute, giving you have some thought regarding which stocks you ought to purchase or utilize a facility that can offer you counsel and direction on such issues.

This methodology is known as a purchase and hold system and can enable you to expand your riches over the long haul, yet it doesn't give a lot, And when anything, in the method for transient increases. Nowadays, numerous speculators are utilizing a progressively dynamic venture style to attempt to make increasingly prompt returns.

On account of the scope of online handles that empower speculators to make exchanges on the stock trades with only a couple of snaps of their mouse, it's moderately direct for financial specialists to be progressively dynamic if they wish to. Numerous individuals exchange online on either low maintenance or a full-time premise, purchasing and selling consistently to attempt to exploit shorter-term value changes and frequently clutching their buys for only half a month or days, or even only several hours.

There are a lot of budgetary instruments that can be effectively exchanged. Options, specifically, have demonstrated to be extremely prevalent among merchants, and options trading is winding up increasingly standard. On this page, we have given some valuable data on what is associated with alternatives exchanging and how it functions.

Indeed, you've got it - alternatives exchanging is just exchanging options, and is commonly finished with protections on the stock or security advertise (only as ETFs and so forth).

First off, you can sell alternatives through a business-like E*Trade (ETFC) or Fidelity (FNF).

When purchasing a call alternatively, the strike cost of a possibility for a stock, for instance, will be resolved dependent on the present price of that stock. For example, if a portion of a given stock (like Amazon (AMZN) is $1,748, any strike value (cost of the call alternative) that is over that offer cost viewed as "out of the cash." Conversely, if the strike cost is under the present offer cost of the stock, it's considered "in cash."

In any case, for put options (appropriate to sell), the inverse is valid - with strike costs underneath the present offer value being considered "out of the cash" and the other way around. Furthermore, what's increasingly significant - any "out of the cash" alternatives (regardless of whether call or put options) are useless at lapse (so you genuinely need to have an "in cash" options when exchanging on the securities exchange).

Another approach to consider it is that call alternatives are commonly bullish, while put options are widely bearish.

Alternatives commonly lapse on Fridays with various periods (for instance, month to month, every other month, quarterly, and so on.). Numerous alternatives agreements are a half year.

How Options Work

As far as esteeming alternative agreements, it is basically about deciding the probabilities of future value occasions. The more probable something is to happen, the more costly an alternative would be that benefits from that occasion. For example, a call worth goes up as the stock (fundamental) goes up. It is the way to understanding the overall estimation of options.

The less time there is until expiry, the less worth an alternative will have. This is because the odds of value move in the underlying stock reduce as we move nearer to expiry. If you purchase a one-month choice that is out of the cash, and the stock doesn't move, the options turn out to be less significant as time passes. Since time is a part of the cost of an alternative, one-month options will be less critical than three-month options. This is because, with additional time accessible, the likelihood of a cost move in support of you increments, and the other way around.

Exchanging Call versus Put Options

Acquiring call options is wagering that the cost of the portion of security (like stock or record) will go up throughout a foreordained measure of time. For example, if you purchase a call option for Alphabet (GOOG) at, state, $1,500, and are feeling bullish about the stock, you are foreseeing that the offer cost for Alphabet will increment.

When buying put options, you are anticipating the cost of the underlying security to go down after some time (in this way, you're bearish on the stock). If you are obtaining put options on the S&P 500 record with a present estimation of $2,100 per share, you are bearish about the financial exchange. You are accepting the S&P 500 will decrease in an incentive over a given timeframe (possibly to sit at $1,700). For this situation, since you acquired the put options when the file was at $2,100 per share (accepting the strike cost was at or in cash), you would have the opportunity to sell the options at that equivalent cost (not the new, lower-cost). I would approach a decent "cha-ching" for you as a financial specialist.

Options exchanging (particularly in the financial exchange) are influenced fundamentally by the cost of the basic security, time until the termination of the options, and the instability of the basic security.

The premium of the options (its cost) is dictated by natural incentives in addition to its time esteem (extraneous worth).

Chronicled versus Suggested Volatility

Instability in options exchanging alludes to how huge the value swings are for a given stock.

Similarly, as you would envision, high instability with protections (like stocks) implies higher hazard - and alternately, low unpredictability means lower chance.

When exchanging options on the securities exchange, stocks with high unpredictability (ones whose offer costs sway a great deal) are more costly than those with low instability (albeit because of the whimsical idea of the financial exchange, even small instability stocks can turn out to be great unpredictability ones in the long run).

Why Use Options?

Recorded unpredictability is a decent proportion of instability since it quantifies how much a stock vacillated every day over a one-year timeframe. Then again, suggested uncertainty is an estimation of the unpredictability of a stock (or security) later on dependently available over the hour of the alternative agreement.

Worth: Time Value and in/at/out of the Money

And when you are purchasing an option that is as of now "in cash" (which means the alternative will quickly be in benefit), its exceptional will have an additional expense since you can sell it promptly for a profit. Then again, if you have an option that is "at the cash," the alternative is equivalent to the present stock cost. Also, as you may have speculated, a choice that is "out of the cash" is one that won't have extra worth since it is right now, not in benefit.

For call alternatives, "in cash" agreements will be those whose fundamental resource's value (stock, ETF, and so forth.) is over the strike cost. For put options, the agreement will be "in cash" if the strike cost is beneath the present cost of the hidden resource (stock, ETF, and so on.).

The time esteem, which is likewise called the outward worth, is the estimation of the alternative over the intrinsic worth (or, over the "in the cash" region).

If an option (regardless of whether a put or call alternative) will be "out of the cash" by its termination date, you can offer options to gather a period premium.

The more extended an alternative has before its lapse date, the additional time it needs to make a benefit, so its top-notch (cost) will be higher because its time worth is higher. On the other hand, the less time an option agreement has before it lapses, the less its time worth will be (the less extra time worth will add to the premium).

In this way, as it were, if an option has a ton of time before it lapses, the more extra time worth will be added to the top-notch (cost) - and the less time it has before termination, the less time worth will be added to the premium.

Upsides and downsides

A portion of the significant masters of alternatives exchanging spin around their alleged security

As per Nasdaq's alternatives exchanging tips, options are regularly stronger to changes (and downturns) in market costs, can help increment salary on present and future ventures can frequently improve bargains on an assortment of values and, maybe above all, can enable you to profit by that value rising or dropping after some time without putting resources into it legitimately.

There are cons to exchanging alternatives - including hazards.

There is an assortment of approaches to decipher dangers related to alternatives exchanging, yet these dangers spin around the degrees of unpredictability or vulnerability of the market. For instance, costly options are those whose vulnerability is high - which means the market is unpredictable for that specific resource, and it is progressively dangerous to exchange it.

Options Trading Strategies

When exchanging options, the agreements will ordinarily take this structure:

Stock ticker (name of the stock), date of termination (usually in mm/dd/yyyy, albeit in some cases times are flipped with the year first, month second and day last), the strike value, call or put, and the top-notch cost (for instance, $3). So a case of a call alternative for Apple stock would look something like this: APPL 01/15/2018 200 Call @ 3.

Contingent upon what stage you are exchanging on, the

alternative exchange will look altogether different.

There are various techniques you can utilize when options were exchanging - all of which fluctuate on hazard, reward, and different elements. And keeping in mind that there are many procedures (the more significant part of them genuinely convoluted), here are a couple of structural systems that have been prescribed for apprentices.

Secured Call

And when you have great resource speculations (like stocks, for instance), a secured call is an incredible alternative for you. This system is commonly useful for speculators who are just nonpartisan or marginally bullish on a stock.

A secured call works by purchasing 100 portions of standard stock and selling one call option for every 100 shares of that stock. This sort of technique can help lessen the danger of your present stock speculations yet additionally gives you a chance to make benefit from the alternative.

Secured calls can profit when the stock cost increments or remains consistent over the hour of the options agreement. Be that as it may, you could lose cash with this sort of exchange if the stock value falls excessively (yet can in reality still profit And when it just falls a smidgen). In any case, by utilizing this technique, you are shielding your venture from reductions in offer cost while allowing yourself the chance to profit while the stock cost is level.

Selling Iron Condors

With this technique, the merchant's hazard can either be moderate or hazardous, relying upon their inclination (which is unmistakable in addition to). For iron condors, the situation of the exchange is non-directional, which means the advantage (like a stock) can either go up or down - along these lines, there is benefit potential for a genuinely wide range. To utilize this sort of system, sell a put and purchase another put at a lower strike cost (basically, a put spread), and consolidate it by buying a call and selling a call at a higher strike value (a call spread). These calls and puts are short.

At the point when the stock value remains between the two puts or calls, you make a benefit (along these lines, when the value changes to some degree, you're profiting). In any case, the procedure loses cash when the stock cost either increments definitely above or drop radically underneath the spreads. Therefore, the iron condor is viewed as an impartial market position.

Options Trading Examples

There are heaps of instances of alternatives exchanging that, to a great extent, rely upon which system you are utilizing. In any case, as a fundamental thought of what an ordinary call or put options would be, we should consider a broker purchasing a call and put an alternative on Microsoft (MSFT).

When you purchased a long call alternative (recollect, a call option is an agreement that gives you the privilege to buy shares later on) for 100 portions of Microsoft stock at $110 per share for December 1, you would reserve the option to purchase 100 pieces of that stock at $110 per share paying little respect to if the stock value changed or not by December 1. For this extended call options, you would expect the cost of Microsoft to increment, consequently giving you a chance to harvest the benefits when you can get it at a less expensive expense than its reasonable worth.

If you choose not to practice that privilege to purchase the offers, you will lose the top-notch you paid for the alternative since you aren't committed to buying any suggestions.

And when you were purchasing a since quite a while ago put options for Microsoft, you would wager that the cost of Microsoft offers would diminish up until your agreement terminates, so that, And whenever you practiced your entitlement to sell those offers, you'd sell them at a more significant expense than their reasonably estimated worth.

Another model includes purchasing a long call option for a $2 premium (so for the 100 offers for every agreement, that would rise to $200 for the entire deal). You purchase a possibility for 100 portions of Oracle (ORCL) at a strike cost of $40 per share, which lapses in two months, anticipating that stock should go to $50 at that point. You've burned through $200 on the agreement (the $2 premium occasions 100 offers for the contract). At the point when the stock value hits $50 as you wager it would, your call alternative to purchasing at $40 per offer will be $10 "in cash" (the agreement is presently worth $1,000 since you have 100 portions of the stock) - since the distinction somewhere in the range of 40 and 50 is 10. Now, you can practice your consider alternative and purchase the stock at $40 per share rather than the $50 it is currently worth - making your $200 unique agreement now worth $1,000 - which is an $800 benefit and a 400% return.

Basic Options Trading Mistakes

There are a lot of missteps; even prepared merchants can make when exchanging options.

One basic mix-up for merchants to make is that they think they have to clutch their call or put alternative until the termination date. If your options' underlying stock goes far up overnight (multiplying your request or put alternative's worth), you can practice the agreement promptly to procure the increases (regardless of whether you have, say, 29 days left for the options).

Another regular error for alternatives brokers (particularly fledglings) is to neglect to make a decent leave plan for your options. For instance, you might need to plan to leave your alternative when you either endure a misfortune or when you've arrived at a benefit that is just as you would prefer (rather than holding out in your agreement until the lapse date).

What does Option Trading Involve?

In fundamental terms, options exchanging includes purchasing and selling options contracts on the open trades and, extensively, it's fundamentally the same as the stock exchange. Though stock merchants expect to make benefits through purchasing stocks and selling them at a more significant expense, options dealers can make benefits through buying alternatives agreements and selling them at a more considerable expense. Likewise, similarly, that stockbrokers can take a short position on stock that they accept will go down in worth, options merchants can also do with alternatives contracts.

By and by, in any case, this type of exchange is more adaptable than stock exchanges. For a specific something, the way that options agreements can be founded on a wide assortment of fundamental protections implies that there is a lot of degree with regards to choosing how and where to contribute. Dealers can utilize alternatives to theorize on the value development of individual stocks, files, remote monetary forms, and items in addition to other things, and this introduces unmistakably more open doors for potential benefits.

The genuine flexibility, however, is in the different options types that can be exchanged.

When exchanging stocks, you fundamentally have two principle methods for profiting through taking either a long position or a short position on a particular stock. If you anticipated that a specific stock should go up in worth, at that point, you would take a long place by purchasing that stock with the end goal of selling it later at a more significant expense. If you anticipated that a specific stock should go down in worth, at that point, you would take a short position by short offering that stock with a want to repurchasing it later at a lower cost.

In alternatives exchanging, there's increasingly decision in the manner in which exchanges can be executed and a lot more approaches to profit.

It ought to be clarified that options exchanging are a substantially more confounded subject than stock exchanges, and the entire idea of what is included can appear to be exceptionally overwhelming to amateurs. There is absolutely a great deal you ought to learn before you begin and contribute your cash. Notwithstanding, the majority of the essentials aren't that hard to understand. When you have gotten a handle on the nuts and bolts, it turns out to be a lot more clear precisely what alternatives exchanging is about.

Beneath, we clarify in more detail all the different procedures included.

Purchasing Options

Purchasing an option agreement is practically speaking indistinguishable to purchasing stock. You are essentially taking a long position on that options, anticipating that it should go up in worth. You can purchase alternatives shrinks by basically picking precisely what you wish to purchase and what number of, and afterward putting in purchase to open request with an agent. This request was named all things considered because you are opening a situation through purchasing alternatives.

If your options do go up in worth, at that point, you can either sell them or exercise your alternative relying upon what suits you best. We give more data on selling and practicing alternatives later.

One of the enormous focal points of options agreements is that you can get them in circumstances when you anticipate that the hidden resource should go up in worth and cases when you expect that the necessary resource should go down.

When anticipating that a hidden resource should go up in worth, at that point, you would purchase call options, which gives you the privilege to acquire the fundamental resource at a fixed cost. If you were anticipating that a vital resource should go down in worth, at that point, you would purchase put options, which gives you the privilege to sell the hidden support at a fixed cost. This is only one case of the adaptability on these agreements; there are a few more.

If you have recently opened a short position on options decreases by thinking of them, at that point, you can likewise repurchase those agreements to close that position. To close a situation by purchasing contracts, you would put in purchase to close requests with your intermediary.

Selling and Writing Options

There are mostly two manners by which you can sell alternatives contracts. Initially, if you have recently purchased agreements and wish to understand your benefits, or cut your misfortunes, at that point, you would offer them by putting in an offer to close request. The request has named all things considered because you are shutting your situation by selling alternatives contracts.

You would ordinarily utilize that request if the options you possessed had gone up in worth and you needed to take your benefits by then, or if the alternatives you claimed had fallen in value. You needed to leave your situation before bringing about some other misfortunes.

The other way you can sell options is by opening a short position and short selling them. This is otherwise called composition alternatives because the procedure includes you composing new agreements sold in the market. When you do this you are assuming the commitment in the contract for example and when the holder practices their options, at that point you would need to sell them the fundamental security at the strike cost (if a call options) or purchase the underlying security from them at the strike cost (if a put alternative).

Composing alternatives is finished by utilizing the offer to open requests, and you would get an installment at the hour of submitting such a request. This is commonly more hazardous than exchanging through purchasing and after that selling, yet there are benefits to be made And when you recognize what you are doing. You would as a rule put in such a request And whenever you accepted the applicable hidden security would not move so that the holder would have the option to practice their options for a benefit.

For instance, And whenever you accepted that a specific stock was going to either stay static or fall in worth, at that point, you could compose and sell call options dependent on that stock.

You would be obligated to potential misfortunes if the stock went up in worth, however, And when it neglected to do as such when the options terminated, you would keep the installment you got for thinking of them.

Practicing Options

Options dealers will, in general, make their benefits through the purchasing, selling, and composing of alternatives instead of ever really practicing them. Notwithstanding, contingent upon the procedures you are utilizing and the reasons you have purchased certain agreements, there might be events when you practice your alternatives to purchase or sell the hidden security.

The straightforward truth that you can conceivably make cash out of practicing just as purchasing and selling them further serves to represent exactly how much adaptability and flexibility this type of exchanging offers.

Options Spreads

What truly makes exchanging options such a fascinating

method to contribute is the capacity to make alternatives spread. You can make cash transferring by purchasing options and after that selling them And when you make a benefit, yet the spreads are the genuinely amazing assets in exchange. A range is essentially when you enter a situation on at least two options agreements dependent on the equivalent fundamental security; for instance, purchasing alternatives on a particular stock and composing arrangements on a similar share.

There are various sorts of spreads that you can make, and they can be utilized for a wide range of reasons. Most regularly, they have utilized as far as possible the hazard associated with taking a position or decreasing the budgetary expense required with taking a position.

Most options exchanging systems include the utilization of spreads. A few methodologies can be exceptionally confused, yet there are additionally various genuinely essential techniques that are straightforward.

Step by step instructions to Buy And Sell Options

It is showcase shrewdness that keen alternative dealers purchase modest options and sell costly options. Furthermore, without a doubt, we often observe that the perfect alternative to purchasing will be very expensive (and in this way dangerous), regardless of the high likelihood of value development. Undoubtedly, the whole idea of secured call composing is worked around that center standard: selling overrated (exaggerated) options to the individuals who overlook this guideline.

Stock Price and Its Effect on Option Values

Since investment opportunities purchased to open all around are purchased to either hypothesize on the stock's development or to fence against the event, it is common that an option's worth will move because of changes in stock cost.

Call esteems move a similar way as the stock and put esteems move contrarily (inverse) to the stock cost. The measure of progress in an option's price will be controlled by the alternative's delta – clarified further on. One who thinks a stock will inescapably rise would purchase a call to conjecture on it; if bearish, a put would be the acquisition of decision.

Purchasing Options

Other than to close a short alternative position, brokers purchase investment opportunities for two essential reasons: to support a current stock position or to hypothesize on the course of the hidden stock. The individuals who anticipate that the stock should go down will purchase puts, either theoretically or fence a long stock position. The individuals who expect that the stock should go up will buy calls, either hypothetically or to a short area in the capital.

Since investment opportunities can be purchased for a small amount of the expense of the underlying stock, yet give the holder the privilege to acquire (calls) or sell (puts) the hidden share whenever through termination, they provide the holder influence over the basic offers for the life of the alternative.

Model: If you pay $100,000 for a six-month call alternative to purchase for $5,000,000, you control the particular thing for the options time frame, for an ostensible entirety. This is an influence. The proprietors of the business can't offer the property to any other person until your options lapses. You can practice the call whenever, sell the options or let it lapse – it's your decision. Unexercised, the request will terminate uselessly.

Theorizing on stock heading by buying alternatives is an old game, and it can work very well. The issue is that the stock must make the ideal move before termination. In this way, the purchaser of the option must get both the course and timing of the stock move right.

Selling Options

Dealers sell investment opportunities principally to create a salary. The system utilized will be managed by whether one is bullish/nonpartisan or bearish (list discards alternative spreads):

· Bullish/Neutral: offer secured calls to produce pay

· Time esteem premium produces returns in any event when the stock itself is level

· Bearish: sell calls bare to exploit stock's disappointment

· Releases exchange to termination or repurchases calls at

a benefit when the stock pulls back

· Bullish/Neutral: sell OTM puts as an option in contrast to a secured call

· Exposed put composing makes a salary, the OTM strike lessens task chance

· Bullish: sell ATM, or even ITM puts into gaining stock at markdown

· The put premium lessens the stock expense whenever relegated; unadulterated benefit if not allowed

Purchasing Options – Strategy

Examiners purchase investment opportunities fundamentally to theorize on a foreseen development in the hidden stock since the options will pick up in an incentive as the stock moves. Examiners don't purchase options when they have a nonpartisan attitude toward the capital, so the technique utilized is directed by whether one is bullish or bearish.

Bullish: purchase calls to profit by the anticipated stock ascent

ITM call is most costly yet gains in cost at the most elevated rate with stock's ascent

ATM call is the best worth, however, doesn't move dollar-for-dollar with the stock

OTM call is least expensive yet factually the most

exceedingly terrible purchase

Bearish: purchase puts into gaining by anticipated stock fall

ITM put is most costly yet gains in cost at the most noteworthy rate with stock's fall

ATM put is the best worth, however, doesn't move dollar-for-dollar with the stock

OTM put is least expensive yet factually the most noticeably awful purchase

If the options' value moves dollar-for-dollar with the stock, the options' delta is 1.0 for a call and - 1.0 for a put. If the alternative moves $0.50 for a dollar move in the stock, the delta is 0.50 for a call and - 0.50 for a put.

Consequently, for instance, when the stock is $45, the 50 Call may cost just $1.00, however with a delta of 0.30, the capital would need to move to about $53 altogether at the call cost to twofold. The stock needs to work a lot harder (move further) to make gainfulness for the ATM or OTM call purchaser. The additional time esteem the purchaser paid, the more the stock must move.

Not all ng alternatives are theoretical. Alternatives are likewise purchased to fence a contradicting position. For instance, one who is short the stock may buy a defensive call to guarantee the capacity to buy the stock at a true cost should the exchange turn out badly (stock goes up). Or then again, one who is long the capital may purchase a defensive put to guarantee the capacity to sell the stock at a real cost should the stock fall.

Time Value

It is essential for anybody composing secured calls or making any alternative based exchanges to comprehend time worth and its significance. For the alternative author, time worth is one of the significant wellsprings of return (the other benefits from sharply exchanging options as the stock moves). In any case, for the alternative holder, time worth is harmful since it rots and picks his pocket over the long haul. Altogether for along options situation to win, the purchaser of the option initially should recover the time an incentive before the exchange can end up productive. For instance, if when the stock is $50, the broker pays $2 for the present 50 Call, which is ATM, and therefore unsurpassed worth, the breakeven point is $52 (50.00 strike cost + 2.00-time esteem). The holder must consider selling the stock for $52 to recover the calls' expense, and just the sum got above $52 will be gain.

It is regularly said that time is the options author's companion and the alternative purchaser's foe. This is valid because time worth rots at an anticipated rate as time slips by.

Time Value in Short Calls

In the secured call, returns produced when a worth bit of the premium. Accept that we purchased a stock for $50 and composed the 45 Call on it for a $6.00 dividend. That is a hefty premium, yet we are committed to selling the stock for $45 whenever called. The time worth is just $1.00 (6.00 – 5.00 of inherent worth).

Whenever got out at $45, our benefit will be the $1.00 of time esteem, in spite of that tremendous call premium, since we are selling the stock at a $5.00 misfortune.

Time Value in Long Options – and How It Is Forfeited

Assume that as opposed to purchasing the stock, we had bought the 45 Call at the expense of $6.00. The call gives us the privilege to buy the stock – presently exchanging at $50 – for $45. Deducting out the $5.00 of special incentive from the calls' cost, we paid $1.00 in time esteem. Be that as it may, if the call instead is worked out, the time worth is discarded.

This exchange would bring about a $1.00 misfortune. By practicing the call, the holder relinquishes the time esteem. Time and incentive for the holder of the option genuinely is a "utilization it or lose it" suggestion. At whatever point an ITM call or put has time esteem, the holder relinquishes the time an incentive upon exercise. Had the alternative holder rather sold the calls for $6, the time worth would have been recovered? In any event, marketing the calls for $5.50 would have yielded a superior outcome than relinquishing all the time esteem.

The main route for the alternative holder to recover the calls' time worth is to sell the options, and the closer lapse draws near, the additional time worth will rot. This outlines why ITM calls are not practiced before termination since, despite everything, they have time esteem. However, when time worth is gone or almost gone, it is never again an obstacle to early call practice, and the call essayist can confront new tasks whenever. If the call exchanges beneath equality (underneath inherent worth), the first exercise turns out to be much almost certain.

Guessing on stock bearing by acquiring alternatives is an old game, and it can work very well. The issue is that the stock must make the ideal move before lapse.

Bullish: sell ATM or even ITM puts to procure stock at rebate

The put premium lessens the stock expense whenever allowed; unadulterated benefit if not relegated.

Purchasing Options – Strategy

Examiners purchase investment opportunities principally to estimate on a foreseen development in the underlying stock since the options will pick up in an incentive as the stock moves. Theorists don't purchase alternatives when they have an impartial attitude toward the capital, so the methodology utilized is directed by whether one is bullish or bearish.

Bullish: purchase calls to profit by the anticipated stock ascent

ITM call is most costly yet gains in cost at a most noteworthy rate with stock's ascent

ATM call is the best worth, yet doesn't move dollar-for-dollar with the stock

OTM call is least expensive however factually the most noticeably awful purchase

Bearish: purchase puts to benefit from anticipated stock fall

ITM put is most costly yet gains in cost at the most elevated rate with stock's fall

ATM put is the best worth, yet doesn't move dollar-for-dollar with the stock

OTM put is least expensive yet factually the most noticeably terrible purchase

And when the options' value moves dollar-for-dollar with the stock, the alternative's delta is 1.0 for a call and - 1.0 for a put. If the option moves $0.50 for a dollar move in the stock, the delta is 0.50 for a call and - 0.50 for a put.

Hence for instance, when the stock is $45, the 50 Call may cost just $1.00, yet with a delta of 0.30, the capital would need to move to about $53 altogether at the call cost to twofold. The stock needs to work a lot harder (push further) to make a benefit for the ATM or OTM call purchaser. The additional time esteem the purchaser paid, the more the stock must move.

Long Option Economics

Here is a significant point about the financial matters of purchasing alternatives: eventually, the holder of the option should either sell or exercise the ITM extended options. Something else, the options will lapse useless. Accept as in the above model that an author paid $6.00 for a $45 consider when the stock is $50. If the holder makes no move by termination, the calls will lapse useless, bringing about the loss of the whole premium paid. And when the stock still is at $50 when lapse moves around, instead of assuming a $6.00 misfortune, the holder could practice the 45 Call to purchase the stock for $45 and sell it at $50, which decreases the disaster to $1.00, as appeared in the time-esteem relinquishment model above.

And when the stock has stayed at $50, at that point near termination the call holder could roll the shouts to the following month by selling the present require its $5 of special incentive in addition to any outstanding time worth and purchasing the next month's 45 Call for around $6. The expense of the roll would be an extra $1 or so of time esteem (really, the distinction among present and one month from now time an incentive for the calls), however, rolling the gets out keeps the broker in the game and abstains from relinquishing the calls' true worth. Rather than assuming a $1.00 misfortune, at that point, the merchant could instead utilize the equivalent $1.00 to roll the gets out one month.

OTM options are never practiced even at termination since it would be unquestionably progressively profitable to purchase or sell the stock at the market.

Futures:

Tips for putting resources into securities exchange - Trading prospects

And when you don't here is a snappy definition, a future is a kind of auxiliary instrument where two gatherings consent to execute a lot of budgetary tools or physical wares for future conveyance at a specific cost.

Here is a more straightforward clarification, suppose you choose to purchase a link membership. You are the purchaser in this model; you go into a concurrence with the link organization to get specific help to a particular cost for the following year. This is like a fates contract; you have consented to get an item at a future date at a specific price and specific terms. You have verified the cost for the present, and regardless of whether the value rises and by going into this agreement, you have discounted your danger of more significant expenses.

The fates market has numerous dangers. However, the possibility to make enormous benefits is significant because of a lot of instability in these business sectors. There is a wide range of prospects markets and systems you can use in them, they are.

Items

Items are physical items whose worth is controlled by market interest. These can incorporate gold, grains, and vitality. One methodology you can use in these business sectors is "Straddles." A straddle is built by holding a

139

similar number of calls (where you guess that the cost will rise) and puts (where you conjecture that the price will fall) with the same strike cost and termination date. The fundamental thought is that you figure the costs will stay unpredictable later on, either going up or down.

Another technique is to purchase a call choice, buy calls when you accept that the cost of the advantage will acknowledge sooner rather than later. Then again, you will obtain a put choice if you take the price will decrease.

Monetary forms

At the point when you exchange monetary standards, you conjecture that the costs of money will rise or fall later on. One methodology utilized is called scalping; this is the point at which you endeavor to make momentary benefits from the gradual changes in the estimation of cash. And when you do this, again and again, you will, in the end, make noteworthy benefits.

Files and loan fees

Timing systems are amazingly famous in these business sectors; double-crossing procedures utilized are cycle and regular exchanging.

Cycle exchanging is finished by examining the recorded date and discovering conceivable here and there cycles for an essential resource. Usually utilized cycles for stock list prospects are the multi-week and multi-day period. Examining the value patterns related to cycles can prompt massive additions for shrewd speculators.

Occasional exchange is the point at which you endeavor to transfer the regular impacts that happen in these business sectors. Verifiable information shows that most markets have comparative examples of a seemingly endless amount of time after year. Thinking about these random patterns is a powerful method to exchange for the benefit.

Another excellent method to begin is by focusing on these four distinct fates showcases; this will fabricate your insight as you learn without expanding your general measure of hazard; at that point, as you incorporate certainty extends with exchanging different sorts of fates.

Futures are investments that allow you to buy commodities by locking in a certain price at a specific time without actually buying the shares. These are speculative bets you are placing on the future price of a commodity, sometimes far in advance. In addition to products such as crude oil and corn, stocks, foreign currencies, and Treasury bonds are also connected to futures and can be traded on various exchanges.

On the one hand, a distinct advantage of locking in a price for an extended period is to mitigate some of the volatility in a particular market. On the other hand, making short-term bets on an increase in price can yield massive returns. Because there are unlimited gains and unlimited losses, this type of investment is typically recommended for savvy and aggressive investors who have extremely high tolerance levels for risk. The examples of investors who use futures generally include hedge funds, wealthy individual investors, and institutions.

With futures contracts, you do not own the shares or the actual commodity. You don't even put down the same amount as if you were purchasing the asset. What is most appealing about futures is the opportunity to gain from short-term shifts in the price of the commodity either based on the movement of the market, often hedging against significant losses in markets that tend to experience more volatility. Despite the risks that accompany futures, most experts agree that they are a reliable diversification tool in addition to, and with different characteristics than stocks and bonds. As a result, they are rapidly growing in popularity with individual investors.

If you are getting your feet wet in futures markets, the first thing you will want to do is to open an account with a broker at a reputable trading firm. Select a futures market that is active easy to liquidate. You will then be required to put down a margin. While you can open an account at a brokerage with just a few thousand dollars, you will need to place a much more significant chunk of cash into a futures trading account to cover any margin calls should the price of the commodity drop. This is needed to cover losses to maintain the minimum amount of funds required as part of your contract.

Individuals can trade their accounts without a broker. This approach increases the risk and requires constant care and attention to trends and predictions. A managed account allows your broker to leverage their expertise and trade on your behalf, reducing the amount of time, concentration, and some degree of risk for you. A third option is to select a commodity pool — that pools together a set of commodities. The benefits of commodity pools are similar to that of mutual funds in that they pool together funds from several investors, investing in several products. These also don't require margin calls. However, the general risks that are inherent in other types of futures trading still exist with commodity pools.

If you are beginning to learn about futures, why not do some paper trades first? Pretend to buy, hold, and sell to see if you come out ahead in the game. This simulation may prevent you from losing lots of real money!

ETFs:

A trade exchanged reserve (ETF) is a sort of security that includes a gathering of protections, for example, stocks—that frequently tracks a hidden list, even though they can put resources into any number of industry divisions or utilize different techniques. ETFs are from numerous points of view like common assets; be that as it may, they are recorded on trades, and ETF offers an exchange for the day only like standard stock.

Kinds of ETFs

There are different kinds of ETFs accessible to financial specialists that can be utilized for money age, hypothesis, cost increments, and to the fence or mostly counterbalance hazard in a speculator's portfolio. The following are a few instances of the kinds of ETFs.

Security ETFs may incorporate government securities,

corporate securities, and state and neighborhood securities—called municipal securities.

Industry ETFs track a specific industry, for example, innovation, banking, or the oil and gas segment.

Product ETFs put resources into items, including unrefined petroleum or gold.

Money ETFs put resources into extreme monetary forms, for example, the Euro or Canadian dollar.

Backward ETFs endeavor to win gains from stock decreases by shorting stocks. Shorting is selling a stock, anticipating a decline in esteem, and repurchasing it at a lower cost.

Financial specialists ought to know that numerous backward ETFs are Exchange Traded Notes (ETNs) and false ETFs. An ETN is a bond yet exchanges like a stock and is upheld by a backer like a bank. Make sure to check with your intermediary to decide whether an ETN is a correct fit for your portfolio.

In the U.S., most ETFs are set up as open-finished assets. They are dependent upon the Investment Company Act of 1940 except where the following guidelines have changed their administrative prerequisites. Open-end assets don't restrain the number of speculators associated with the item.

Step by step instructions to Buy and Sell ETFs

ETFs exchange through online intermediaries and customary intermediary sellers.

You can see a portion of the top specialists in the business for ETFs with Investopedia's rundown of the best agents for ETFs. An option in contrast to standard dealers is Robo-counsels like Betterment and Wealthfront who utilize ETFs in their speculation items.

Preferences and Disadvantages of ETFs

ETFs, give lower ordinary expenses since it would be costly for a financial specialist to purchase every one of the stocks held in an ETF portfolio exclusively. Financial specialists need to execute one exchange to buy and one transaction for selling, which prompts less intermediary commissions since there are just a couple of exchanges being finished by speculators. Representatives usually charge a commission for each trade. A few agents even offer no-commission exchanging on absolute ease ETFs diminishing expenses for financial specialists significantly further.

An ETF's cost proportion is the expense to work and deal with the store. ETFs commonly have low costs since they track a file. For instance, if an ETF tracks the S&P 500 record, it may contain each of the 500 stocks from the S&P, making it an inactively overseen reserve and less time-escalated. Be that as it may, not all ETFs track a record in an inactive way.

Creation

At the point when an ETF needs to give special offers, the A.P. purchases portions of the stocks from the record, for example, the S&P 500 followed by the store—and sells or trades them to the ETF for new ETF shares at an equivalent worth. Like this, the A.P. sells the ETF partakes in the market for a benefit. The procedure of A.P. offering stocks to the ETF support, as a byproduct of offers in the ETF, is called creation.

The most common errors not to commit

Stay away from These Common Mistakes When Investing In ETFs

ETFs, which are crates of stocks, securities, or products that are exchanged on a stock trade, is turning into an undeniably mainstream approach to contribute particularly with youthful speculators. Because of their availability, moment expansion, straightforwardness, low costs, charge proficiency, and capacity to be exchanged like individual stocks, a few specialists even think they'll, in the end, make customary common supports out of date.

In any case, there are drawbacks to know about as well. And when you have ever heard the saying "your most prominent quality can be your shortcoming also," at that point, you will perceive any reason why the accompanying errors can crawl up on an ETF financial specialist if they don't know about them.

Misstep: not changing how you contribute your cash

Numerous individuals put by storing a set sum into their speculation account each month (dollar-cost averaging methodology), which they use to purchase common assets. This can be a slip-up with ETFs since you pay a commission for each purchase and sale request you place which implies that commission costs will diminish your month to month speculation. (Note: this could be discredited And when you are with an online business firm that gives free exchanges.)

Slip-up: losing the focal point of your long haul methodology

ETFs are, for the most part, seen as a long haul speculation holding. Still, since of the advantage of having the option to exchange it (as regularly as intra-day), an error could be made if the financial specialist gets enticed to purchase and undercut with all the more a term viewpoint (read: showcase timing) which can bring about selling at an inappropriate time and having higher exchanging costs and duties.

Misstep: not looking into how an ETF differentiates your portfolio

This can neutralize you in two different ways:

Repetition. For instance, by putting resources into an ETF that tracks the S&P 500 and holding an enormous top shared reserve, you are putting resources into basically a similar sort of stock, and customarily the two speculations will hold similar organizations.

Liquidity danger of specific ETFs. The other miscue is if your ETF is put resources into a particular segment, for instance, in an Antarctic oil sands benchmark (I'm developing a portion), you may experience issues selling your offers when you need.

Mix-up: exchanging "over your head."

"Because a procedure exists doesn't mean you have to utilize it."

One of the benefits of putting resources into ETFs is the adaptability of how they are exchanged and the various methodologies that can be utilized. For instance, one procedure is to "short-sell" an ETF. This methodology is utilized by speculators who accept the cost of their ETF will go down. The speculator, as a result, obtains shares from the business firm, and after that will compensation back the acquired offers with the less expensive offers – expecting the cost does in actuality go down.

Sounds simple right? Not a chance! This is a training that lone experienced speculators may utilize and keeping in mind that the reward (a better yield) could be decent; the hazard is extremely high.

Great guideline affirming principle: in light of the fact that a system exists doesn't really mean you have to utilize it.

At long last, if you inevitably choose to put resources into ETFs, by and large, it's best when you have a singular amount to contribute as that will help limit exchanging costs (see botch 1). Numerous ETFs will have low least speculation prerequisites (could be as low as $250) yet be cautious; an exceptionally low least venture may require a month to month stores, which, as a result of commission expenses, could consume your general return.

Real Estate:

The land is mainstream speculation. There are numerous alterations in the financial framework having puffed-up hazard or lesser returns; the commercial venture center goes on with the arrangement innovative and attractive thinking draws near. These advancements make it significant for land licenses to have necessary and cutting-edge information on land ventures. This doesn't imply that licenses should go about as venture guides. For all the time, they ought to allude speculators to proficient assessment bookkeepers, lawyers, or venture experts. These are the experts who can offer master guidance on a financial specialist's particular needs.

Investing in Real Estate: Factors to consider

The three variables of putting resources into land are region, discernment, and financial aspects. The way to making the best interest in and, and explicitly in cooperatives, and townhouses, is to consider all the three variables. Putting resources into land compare to specific duties concerning the buyer. Interest in the ground made exclusively upon the area of the property won't yield those outcomes. Before making speculation, it is essential to incorporate the three contemplations o Consider in general zone.

o Consider familiarity with the zone.

o Consider the budgetary components.

Real Estate Investment: Benefits

Land esteems have fluctuated widely in different regions of the nation. However, numerous land speculations have appeared better than expected paces of return, for the most part, more noteworthy than the predominant financing costs charged by contract loan specialists. In suspicion, this implies the financial specialist can use the impact of leased cash to contribute a land buy and feel relatively sure that, whenever held long enough, the benefit will yield more money than it cost to fund the buy.

The land offers financial specialists more prominent power over their ventures than make different choices, for example, stocks and so on. Land financial specialists, likewise, are given guaranteed expense focal points.

The most common errors not to commit in real estate

1. Detach Between Real Estate Decisions and Overall Business Strategy

The most significant thing you should remember when occupied with a business land choice is that the choice you are making isn't about land, it's about your business. You're not renting/buying space—you're developing your business.

The greatest mix-up made by little and mid-showcase organizations is the inability to completely adjust and associate land choices within the general business procedure. Indeed, even organizations with as meager as 2,500 sq. Ft. of space can increase noteworthy operational, money related, and promoting focal points by adopting a key strategy.

2. Inability to Understand the Market

With the Internet today, it is simpler than any time in recent memory to think you have a comprehension of the market. In only seconds you can perceive what space is accessible and even how much space is renting or selling for.

This has had two adverse outcomes:

Outfitted with this data, entrepreneurs and administrators have been hushed into a misguided feeling of certainty.

Furthermore, land merchants have gotten self-satisfied. It's simpler than any time in recent memory to force reams of information, print out huge amounts of pictures, and present the presence of learning. While this has helped realtors close business, it's stinging their customers.

3. Mistaking Direct Costs for Total Cost of Occupancy

It appears to be basic enough; include your yearly lease/contract installments, include any form out, and include the expense of utilities and upkeep. When you include these variables, you discover the space that meets your requirements and has the least "cost." As with most business standards, what seems straightforward and clear is normally not successful.

Bonds:

When putting resources into relationships, it's essential to:

Realize when bonds develop. The development date is the date when your speculation will be reimbursed to you. Before you submit your assets, realize to what extent your thinking will be tied up in the bond.

Know the bond's appraising. A relationship's evaluating means that how financially sound it is. The lower the rating, the more hazard there is that the bond will default – and you lose your speculation. AAA is the most noteworthy rating (utilizing the Standard and Poor's appraising framework). Any relationship with a grade of C or beneath is viewed as low quality or garbage bond and has the most noteworthy danger of default.

Examine the bond guarantor's reputation. Knowing the foundation of an organization can be useful when choosing whether to put resources into their bonds.

Comprehend your resistance for the chance. Securities with a lower FICO score commonly offer a better return to make up for more elevated levels of hazard. Ponder your hazard resistance and abstain from contributing exclusively dependent on yield.

The three significant kinds of securities are corporate, metropolitan, and Treasury securities:

Corporate securities are obligation instruments given by an organization to raise capital for activities like extension, innovative work. The premium you win from corporate securities is assessable. Be that as it may, corporate securities usually offer better returns than government or civil securities to balance this drawback.

Municipal securities are given by a city, town, or state to fund-raise for open tasks, for example, schools, streets, and emergency clinics. In contrast to corporate securities, the premium you procure from city securities is tax-exempt. There are two kinds of city bonds: general commitment and income.

<u>CONCLUSION</u>

In any case, a sizeable extent of the rest of forex exchanging is theoretical with merchants working up speculation, which they wish to sell at some phase for benefit. While money may increment or diminish in worth comparative with a broad scope of monetary standards, all forex exchanging exchanges depend on cash sets. In this way, the Euro might be 'solid' against a bushel of financial standards, and merchants will trade only one money pair and may worry about the Euro/U.S. Dollar (EUR/USD) proportion. The changes in relative estimations of monetary standards might be slow or activated by explicit situations, for example, are developing at the hour of composing this - the poisonous obligation emergency.

With straddles (long in this model), you as a dealer are anticipating the advantage (like a stock) to be profoundly unpredictable; however, don't have the foggiest idea about the bearing wherein it will go (up or down). When utilizing a straddle system, you, as the merchant, are purchasing a call and put options at a similar strike cost, hidden cost, and expiry date. This system is regularly utilized when a broker is anticipating the supply of a specific organization to plunge or skyrocket, generally following an occasion like an income report. For instance, when an organization like Apple (AAPL) is preparing to discharge their second from last quarter income on July

31st, An option merchant could utilize a straddle system to purchase a call options to terminate on that date at the present Apple stock cost, and furthermore purchase a put options to lapse around the same time at a similar price.

For chokes (long in this model), a speculator will purchase an "out of the cash" call, and an "out of the cash" put all the while for a similar expiry date for the equivalent essential resource. Financial specialists who utilize this system are accepting the fundamental support (like a stock) will have an emotional value development; however, they don't know in which heading. What causes a long to choke a to some degree safe exchange is that the financial specialist needs the stock to move more noteworthy than the all-out premium paid, yet it doesn't make a difference where bearing.

The upside of a choke procedure is that there is less danger of misfortune since the premiums are more affordable because of how the options are "out of the cash" - which means they're less expensive to purchase.

OPTIONS TRADING FOR BEGINNERS

A Crash Course in Simple Ready-to-Use Strategies to Create Your Passive Income Fortune by Investing in Forex and the Stock Market

By

Benjamin White

TABLE OF CONTENTS

INTRODUCTION

The history of human beings has been mostly the history of slavery. By this, I mean that Man, throughout history, has been a slave: a physical slave, a mental slave, or a financial slave.

A physical slave when Roman empires existed, ships leaving the African continent, shackles, galleys, plantations.

A mental slave when he has been subject to the control of governments, states, feudal lords, and various institutions that have tamed and domesticated him so that others could carry out their agendas.

And a financial slave, which is the subtlest form of slavery that exists, when you apparently enjoy the income you receive, but you are dispossessed of that money in various ways wisely orchestrated by the elites (among which you do not include yourself, of course): rates that they are created because yes, abusive taxes, bank interests, penalties for late payment, debts (other person!) that you have to pay (and that no matter how much you pay, you always owe), etc.

There may be people who do not share this approach, but I remember that, as someone said, there is no higher jail than that in which the bars are not seen. To tame the masses, you have to convince them that they are free.

Lately, in the most recent decades, everything has been changing. There is a revolution of consciousness that operates on many levels: personal, spiritual, social, political, environmental, and also, of course, financial.

In this last field, let's say that there are people who are beginning to realize that, perhaps, no matter how hard they work, they never have anything. That others take everything and that one, go to God! It is getting worse.

So they begin to take the reins of their lives and decide what to do at all times (and for the future), regardless of what they have always done or what they have always been told. They begin, say, to be free (oh!!!, a beautiful word, we start to enter into the matter).

Financially and economically speaking, passive income has much to say here. In the next chapter, we will see precisely what they consist of, but for now, you should know that they have a lot to do with words such as independence, freedom, comfort, fluency, self-responsibility, income, etc.

If you resonate with this, we can continue together. If you are afraid of these words, perhaps it would be better if you return to your comfort zone (we all have one, and very nice, as the name implies).

In recent decades, the books of Robert Kiyosaki have become popular, which have titles whose words include those of comfortable retreat, money flow, a conspiracy of the precious, rich child, smart child, etc. etc. And it speaks of passive income and of building automated systems that allow obtaining constant flows of income so as not needed to go to another place to work.

In the same vein, Timothy Ferriss wrote *The Four-Hour Work Week*, taking a radical turn to the thinking of many people. The approach is essentially to live longer and work less. That is, admit that it may not be worth spending a lifetime of work to start living when you retire (assuming you can do it, of course). There is the possibility of working less, earning equal or more, and starting to live from now, without postponing it to the ever-uncertain future.

All these approaches revolve around the idea of passive income. A lot has been written about it; it is a trending topic on some websites, but something fundamental, I think, is missing: a complete and exhaustive list with all the variety of existing and possible passive income sources. I have been studying the subject for years and putting into practice several of them, and I have not found any material or publication that includes a full catalog. Then I decided to create it. And I offer it to you today, here, for your enjoyment and, above all, so that if you wish, you can put it into practice.

To want is 'Power', to want is the first step to 'Achievement', so if you want, go ahead!

CHAPTER 1

WHAT IS AN OPTION

Option contracts usually refer to the purchase or sale of certain assets.

An option is a contract between two parties (a buyer and a seller), in which whoever buys the option acquires the right to exercise what the agreement indicates, although he will not have an obligation to do so.

Option contracts commonly refer to the purchase or sale of certain assets, which may be stocks, stock indices, bonds, or others. These contracts also establish that the operation must be carried out on a pre-established date (in the case of the European ones, since those of the US are exercised at any time) and at a fixed price at the time the contract is signed.

To purchase an option to buy or sell it is necessary to make an initial disbursement (called "premium"), whose value depends, fundamentally, on the price that the asset, that is the object of the contract, has on the market, on the variability of that price and of the period of time between the date on which the contract is signed and the date on which it expires.

Call and Put

The options that grant the right to buy are called 'Call', and those that allow the right to sell are called 'Put'. Additionally, it is called European options that can only be exercised on the date of exercise and American options that can be used at any time during the life of the contract.

When the time comes for the buying party to exercise the option, if it does, two situations occur:

Whoever appears as the seller of the option will be obliged to do what the said contract indicates; that is, sell or buy the asset to the counterparty, in case it decides to exercise its right to buy or sell.

Who appears as the option buyer will have the right to buy or sell the asset. However, if it does not suit you, you can refrain from making the transaction.

An option contract usually contains the following specifications:

- ***Exercise date:*** the expiration date of the right included in the option.
- ***Exercise price:*** agreed price for the purchase/sale of the asset referred to in the contract (called underlying asset).
- ***Option premium or price:*** amount paid to the counterparty to acquire the right to buy or sell.
- **Rights acquired with the purchase of an option:** they can be *Call* (right of purchase) and *Put* (right of sale).
- **Types of Option:** there may be Europeans, which are only exercised on the date of exercise or American, to be used at any time during the contract. There are, besides, other more complex types of options, the so-called *"Exotic Options."*

In international financial markets, the types of options that are traded on organized exchanges are typically American and European. In Chile, as with futures, there is no stock market for options.

Practical example

Purchase of a call option by an importing company to secure the Euro price on that day.

To better understand the use of options, this example is presented by an importing company that wants to ensure against increases in the price of the Euro.

To do so, you can buy a European call option today that gives you the right to buy a million euros, within three months, at $ 550 per euro. To acquire that right, the company pays $ 2 per euro, that is, the option premium has a cost of $ 2,000,000.

If on the expiration date of the option, the price of the euro in the market is over $ 550 (for example, at $ 560), the company will exercise the option to buy them, as it will only pay $ 550 per euro.

On the contrary, if on that date the market price of the Euro was below $ 550 (for example at $ 530), the company will not exercise the option, since it makes no sense to pay $ 550 per euro when it can be purchased at the market at $ 530; In this case, the option expires without being exercised.

The cash flows are as follows:

Today (April 10, 20XX).

Buy a European call option, which gives you the right to

buy USD 1,000,000 to $ 550 on October 10, 20XX, as the value of the premium is 2 and 1,000,000 contracts are purchased (which means that the notional of the agreement is the US $ 1) there is a cash outlay of $ 2,000,000 for that concept ..

Expiration date (October 30, 20XX)

If the Euro is above the exercise price of the option, it would be exercised, and $ 550 per euro will be paid, that is, $ 550,000,000.

Otherwise, the option expires if it is used, and the euros are acquired in the market.

The euros purchased are used to cancel the importation of goods or services:

The following table shows the result of the operation. As can be seen, if on the expiration date of the option contract, the market exchange rate is lower than the exercise price of the call option, the importer will end up paying the market price per euro plus the cost of the premium (in strict rigor, the value of the premium should be updated for the interest that would have been earned if, instead of paying the value of the premium, that money had been deposited); otherwise, the cost of each euro will be equal to the exercise price plus the premium. That is, the importer will have made sure to pay a maximum of $ 552 per euro.

Market exchange rate A	The exercise price of the option	Prima C	Value of the options (1) $D = (A - B)$	Result of the options (2) $E = D - C$	Disbursement for purchase of euros (3) F	Total disbursement $G = F + C$
530	550	2,000,000	0	-2,000,000	530,000,000	532,000,000
540	550	2,000,000	0	-2,000,000	540,000,000	542,000,000
550	550	2,000,000	0	-2,000,000	550,000,000	552,000,000
560	550	2,000,000	10,000,000	8,000,000	550,000,000	552,000,000
570	550	2,000,000	20,000,000	18,000,000	550,000,000	552,000,000
580	550	2,000,000	30,000,000	28,000,000	550,000,000	552,000,000

Notes:

1. On the expiration date, when the price of the euro in the market is lower than the exercise price, the value of the call option will be zero (as it is not appropriate to exercise the purchase right), whereas, if the opposite occurs, the value of the call option will correspond to the difference between those two prices.

2. That result represents how much money was paid or saved by the fact of coverage.

3. Currencies are acquired in the market when it is not optimal to exercise the option, or by exercising the right of

purchase when exercising that right is an optimal decision.

Finally, it should be noted that if a forward-type contract with the same delivery price had been used to perform the same coverage, the importer would have ended up always paying $ 550. However, it would not have had the opportunities (which may appear when hedging with call options) to benefit from declines in the market exchange rate. Also note that the operation is much simpler to perform: a premium is paid at the time of purchasing the option and on the expiration date (or at any time before that date if the option were of the American type) at least the price that has been agreed.

How The Options Work

Option operators must understand the complexity that surrounds them. The knowledge of the operation of the options allows operators to make the right decisions and offers them more options when executing a transaction.

Indicators:

- The value of an option consists of several elements that go hand in hand with the "Greeks":
- The price of the guaranteed value
- Expiration
- Implied volatility
- The actual exercise price
- Dividends
- Interest rates

The "Greeks" provide valuable information on risk management and help rebalance the portfolios to achieve the desired exposure (e.g., delta coverage). Each Greek measures the reaction of the portfolios to small changes in an underlying factor, which allows the individual risks to be examined:

- The delta measures the rate of change of the value of an option regarding changes in the price of the underlying asset.
- The gamma measures the rate of change in the delta in relation to the changes suffered by the price of the underlying asset.
- Lambda or elasticity refers to the percentage change in the value of an option compared to the percentage change in the price of the underlying asset, which offers a method of calculating leverage, also known as "indebtedness".
- Theta calculates the sensitivity of the option value over time, a factor known as "temporary wear."
- Vega measures the susceptibility of the option of volatility. Vega measures the value of the option based on the volatility of the underlying asset.
- Rho represents the sensitivity of the value of an option against variations in the interest rate and measures the value of the option based on the risk-free interest rate.

Therefore, the Greeks are reasonably simple to determine if the Black Scholes model (considered the standard option valuation model) is used and is very useful for intraday and derivatives traders. Delta, theta, and vega are useful tools to measure time, price, and volatility. The value of the option is directly affected by maturity and volatility if:

- For a long period before expiration, the value of the purchase and sale option tends to rise. The opposite situation would occur if, for a short period before expiration, the value of the purchase and sale options is prone to a fall.
- If the volatility increases, so will the value of the purchase and sale options, while if the volatility decreases, the value of the purchase and sale options decreases.
- The price of the guaranteed value causes a different effect on the value of the purchase options than on that of the sale options.
- Usually, as the price of the securities increases, so do the current purchase options that correspond to it, increasing its value while the sale options lose value.
- If the price of the value falls, the opposite happens, and the current purchase options usually experience a drop in value while the value of the sale options increases.

A bonus of options

It happens when an operator acquires an option contract and pays an initial amount to the seller of the option contract. The option premium will vary depending on when it was calculated and on which market options its acquisition was made. The premium may be different within the same market based on the following criteria:

What option has been chosen, in-, at-, or out-of-the-money? An in-the-money option will be sold for a higher premium since the contract is already profitable, and the buyer has direct access to the benefits obtained from the contract. Instead, at- or out-of-the-money options can be purchased for a lower premium.

What is the value of the contract over time?

Once an option contract expires, it loses its value. Therefore, it is logical that the longer the validity period, the higher the premium. This is because the deal has additional temporary costs and that more time is available in which the option can be profitable.

What level of volatility does the market have? The premium will be higher if the options market is more volatile as it increases the possibility of obtaining a more significant benefit from the option. The opposite principle applies to the lower volatility that implies a lower premium as the market is considered relatively 'stable'. The volatility of the options market is determined by using different price scales (the long-term, recent, and expected price scales are the required data) to a selection of price volatility models.

The sale and purchase options do not have equivalent values when they reach their mutual ITM, ATM, and OTM exercise price due to the direct and opposite effects caused by their oscillation in irregular distribution curves, which unbalances them.

Exercises - The number of exercises and increments between the exercises are decided on the basis of the change that is applied to the product.

Option valuation models

It is essential to know the differences between historical

and implicit volatility when applied for stock market purposes.

Historical volatility calculates the movement rate of the underlying asset in a given period of time in which the standard annual deviation of price changes is given as a percentage. Historical volatility is the retrospective measurement at the date of calculation of the information available on the degree of instability of the underlying asset in a given number of trading days (modifiable period) and during a selected period.

The implied volatility is the future approximation of the stock exchange volume of the underlying asset that measures the expected variation in the standard daily deviation of the asset between the date on which it is calculated and the maturity of the option. When analyzing the value of an option, implied volatility is one of the critical factors that an operator has to consider. To calculate implied volatility, an option valuation model is used, taking into account the cost of the option premium.

There are three types of theoretical valuation models that intraday traders use most frequently as an aid to assess implied volatility. These models are the Black-Scholes, the Bjerksund-Stensland, and the Binomial. With them, the calculation is done using algorithms, usually buy and sell options are used at-the-money or nearest-the-money.

The Black-Scholes model is the most used with European options (these options may only be executed on the day of expiration).

The Bjerksund – Stensland model is very efficient if applied to US options that can be executed at any time between the acquisition of the contract and its expiration.

The Binomial model is appropriately applied to American, European, and Bermuda options. Bermuda's are a midpoint between European and American companies and can be executed only on certain days of the contract or on the expiration date.

Types of options

There are two main kinds of options:

1. Selling options: A put option is an option contract that gives the owner the right, but not the obligation, to sell a specified amount of an underlying security at a given price within a certain period of time. This is the opposite of a purchase option, which provides the holder with the right to buy shares.

A sale option becomes more valuable as the price of the underlying share depreciates relative to the exercise price. On the contrary, a sale option loses its value as the underlying share appreciates and its maturity approaches.

The value of a sale option decreases with time since the chances of the stock falling below the specified strike price are less and less with time.

2. The purchase options: A call option is an agreement that gives the investor the right, but not the obligation, to buy stocks, bonds, commodities, or other instruments at a specified price within a specific period of time.

A purchase option gives you the right to buy an asset. You get benefits with a purchase option when the underlying asset increases in price. For example, if a share is priced at $ 50 and you buy your purchase option for $ 50, then you have the right to buy that share for $ 50 regardless of its price as long as the time period has not defeated. Even if the stock goes up to $ 100, you still have the right to buy that stock for $ 50.

The underlying asset

Traditionally, most options have been based on shares of publicly traded companies. However, options based on other underlying investments are increasingly common. This includes options based on stock indices, traded funds (ETF), REIT (real estate investment funds), foreign exchange, and raw materials such as agricultural or industrial products. When it comes to stock option contracts, it is essential to keep in mind that they are based on 100 shares of the underlying value.

An exception would be when there are adjustments by the division of shares or mergers. It is also important to remember that the purchase of stock options is entirely different from the purchase of shares. American options can be exercised at any time between the purchase date and the expiration date. European options can only be redeemed on the due date. Most stock options traded on the stock market are American.

Types of Options:

- Options near month in-the-money
- Protective Sale
- Weekly Options
- Mini Options
- Index Options
- Mini Index Options
- Binary Options

- Futures Options
- Weekly Options EN
- E-Mini Options
- ETF Options
- IRA Accounts

Advantages and Disadvantages of Options

The capital market is full of opportunities as well as risks. To increase chances and minimize risks, private investors should steadily expand and improve their repertoire of financial products that they control. An often unjustifiably neglected instrument are options, partly because of false prejudices and partly because of confusion, options are almost always considered as dangerous and highly risky tools for investing or even compared to gambling. But the truth is quite different: Although options can be wrongly traded and invested at high risk, they often also serve as a hedge or offer the opportunity to seize opportunities with little capital. The pros and cons of options must be disclosed, so you too can benefit as an options investor.

The Main Advantages Of Options

If you look at the various options that the capital market offers to private investors, you will quickly discover that all instruments have their advantages and disadvantages. It is the same with options. Hence, it is quite useful to familiarize yourself with the essential benefits of options before your endeavors with them.

The most significant advantage for many investors is the possibility of being able to set prices without any problems. A short sale with stock lending or the opening of an account with a foreign broker is therefore unnecessary. Put options are suitable for earning on falling courses. You can even decide to go "short" by writing options on rising prices (call options), assuming that prices fall. Another popular feature of options is low capital requirements. Due to the nature of the option, which is just a right to buy an underlying asset, an investment can be made with a much smaller capital investment, which would hardly be possible, for example, directly into the underlying asset. So, about a hundred call options on a particular stock are far cheaper than buying the stock itself a hundred times. Closely associated with this benefit is the leverage effect of options. Depending on the features of the option, the value of the option increases or falls disproportionately to the performance of the underlying. This is a potential benefit for the investor, but it can quickly turn into a downside if the investment is negative.

As a buyer and thus an option holder, you only acquire rights but no obligations. The risk is only in the amount of invested capital, a purchase obligation, or similar outcomes in any case.

Disadvantages Of Options

As always, about investments and the capital market, opportunities and risks together form an inseparable pair. It is the same with options. In short, the biggest risk and, therefore, the biggest drawback of options has already been mentioned: the risk of loss, which is much higher for options, albeit in limited amounts, than for direct investments in the underlying.

This sounds complicated, but on closer inspection, it is not, which can be illustrated sufficiently by an example:

Suppose a stock X stands at 100 euros, and an investor considers this course too low. He, therefore, buys call options on the underlying X low, for example, 100 euros as the exercise price. In the future, however, the value of the X share falls to 95 euros, and even on the expiration date of its options, the situation has not improved. The options have thus become worthless, and he has lost 100 percent of his invested capital. On the other hand, if he had bought the X share directly, the investor would have lost only 5 percent of his capital. He would have had to do a lot more but could keep the stock long-term and wait for a recovery. Options are riskier because the expected movement must occur in the period up to the expiration date. An investor saves a lot of capital when doing so.

Another disadvantage of options is the *'Bundling'* of the underlying assets. Options are typically sold as contracts where multiple options are bundled. So the purchase of a single option on a share is the exception and only rarely possible. With more expensive stocks, this, in turn, brings with it a need for capital that contradicts the basic idea and strategy of options trading.

The most significant advantages at a glance:

- With options, investors can participate and earn comparatively easily both in rising and falling prices.
- Unlike stocks, investors can issue options or "write" options.
- The capital requirements for options trading are much lower than for direct investments in the corresponding underlying.
- This lower capital investment results in a lever

which, of course, becomes an advantage in the case of positive investment.

- As an option owner, you have only acquired rights; it does not follow any obligation to buy or the like.

The most significant disadvantages at a glance:

- If an option remains out of the money until the expiration date, the investor suffers a complete loss.
- The lever, which becomes an advantage on a positive course, has a negative effect to the detriment of the investor.
- Options are bundled sold as contracts and are therefore not always handled as flexibly as shares.

Is there an additional funding option?

A term that haunts time and again through news and social media, without being familiar to all private investors, is the obligation to make additional payments. It is a red cloth for many investors because here, it threatens unlimited loss. At least now, the attention should be one hundred percent, because the unlimited loss is to be understood literally. Theoretically, any loss is possible with an additional funding obligation.

But when trading options, there is, in most cases, no additional funding. Buyers of options, in particular, are not threatened with additional funding. Their risk is limited to the capital required to buy the options, whether put or call options. If an investor chooses falling prices and the price goes up and up, his option is just out of the money and expires on the expiration date. The same applies to investors who have speculated on rising prices: If the price collapses, the option expires on the expiry date; further costs can never arise.

A margin requirement threatens only the issuer, i.e., the seller (also called writer) of options - and that only in an exceptional case: If an issuer offers options on shares that he does not own at this time, he theoretically has an unlimited risk too. Assuming that one share costs 100 euros and the premium for a call option issued is 10 euros, then the writer would make losses for 110.01 euros. If he did not have the stock in his possession but would have to buy it in the event of exercise first, he would later have to buy this at an arbitrarily high price to then pass it to the option buyer for 100 euros. In this case, there would be an unlimited obligation to make additional payments. Especially for beginners, it is recommended either to only resort to the purchase of options or to offer only options on shares that are in their possession. One speaks in such cases of covered calls.

CHAPTER 2

WHY USE THE OPTIONS?

In some cases, the use of options may limit the losses of investment or earn more than by trading inequities directly.

Here are two reasons why some investors opt for options:

• The speculation

Speculation can be thought of as a bet on the evolution of the market price of an asset. The advantage of the options is that you can generate capital gains independently regardless of the direction of the stock price. Given the volatility of the options, it is also possible to win when the stock market falls or goes on the spot.

Speculating on options is a very risky operation. Why?

Because by buying an option, the investor must not only correctly determine in which direction the action will evolve but also the amplitude of this fluctuation. And time is running out, and the option has an expiry date!

But why are speculators interested in options if it is so difficult to profit from them? The answer is simple: the leverage effect. When a single contract controls 100 securities, a small change in the price of the underlying considerably increases capital gains.

• *The cover*

Coverage, or *"hedging,"* is another possible use of

the options. It works a bit like insurance. You can insure your car or your home, but you can also provide your stock market with the help of options.

Some question the merits of the strategy of hedging options by pointing out that it is unwise to invest if one is not sure of his choices.

However, even though large institutions mostly use hedging strategies, a private investor can take advantage of options to hedge their portfolio.

Imagine, for example, that you want to take advantage of the potential offered by a particular CAC40 company while neutralizing your exposure to the index. Well, the options allow you to do it.

Development Of The Option

Options belong to the group of financial derivatives. These are standardized trading instruments. The price development of basic security is the measure for the later price. In the case of derivatives, equities, indices, currencies, or even the derivatives themselves may form the underlying. When traded on the stock exchange, investors most often encounter derivatives in the form of options or futures. These forms of investment are among the most traded products on the stock market. But, what is it exactly, and how did the option develop until the speculative derivative emerged as the currently valid trading tool?

- Options are traded on the stock exchange
- The option is a variant of the derivative
- Derivatives may be based on different titles
- Basic title is authoritative for the later price

The classic option offers the right to trade a commodity at a price called *the strike price*. Both the acquisition (call) and the sale (put) may be considered. Trading does not constitute an obligation, which means that the trader does not need to buy or sell the stock or any other underlying asset. It is merely a matter of justifying the right to trade a commercial product at the pre-determined price at a later date. To acquire the option, the investor pays the seller, who is also called the *writer*, a *premium*, namely the option price; A call warrant thus includes securitization on the right to buy the underlying asset. If you trade the American variation, you, as a buyer, can exercise your option right at any time until the due date.

On the other hand, you can exercise your right in the European version only on the due date. In most circumstances, investors will only exercise the call or put if the price of the underlying at the time of maturity is above or below the base value. Otherwise, the investor should trade the security at a better price in the market. For Call and Put, there are the following profiles:

- Call: Purchase Option - Right to buy the underlying asset
- Put: Put option - Right to sell the underlying asset
- Long: Viewpoint Buyer - buyer position
- Short: Viewing Angle Seller - Verkaufspositon

Note: *Buyers* and *Sellers* refer to the option and not to the underlying asset.

The purchase warrant (call): set on rising prices

The above can best be described by way of example: An investor acquires a warrant of purchase from a bank, also known as an issuer, on a Siemens AG security. This has a base price of 109 euros. The option type is American in this case, and the term has been set to six months. The trader thus has the right to demand from the bank the delivery of the share of Siemens AG at the price of 109 euros. If the paper of Siemens AG is now listed at 120 euros after some time, it is worthwhile for the investor to buy the share at the price of 109 euros. However, should the Siemens share fall to 90 euros, it is cheaper for the investor to buy the security on the market. Therefore, he becomes the option right expire and buys the stock directly on the stock exchange.

However, it remains questionable whether this action also brings the investor a profit. The answer to this question depends primarily on how high the option premium was. Put the case, and the buyer paid a premium of five euros on the right to buy the paper by the due date for 109 euros. In the case of options expiration, the trader has at least made a loss of five euros. When making a purchase, however, he only makes a profit when the underlying asset rises above 109 euros plus the premium, i.e., to more than 114 euros. Under such circumstances, investors may be able to profit indefinitely from rising prices through such a warrant. If the price falls, the loss remains limited to the option premium.

How are warrant options different?

Both options, as well as warrants, are financial instruments with which future transactions are carried out. That's what they have in common with futures. Investors act in these transactions, so to speak, on the development of the option or the warrant. Because trade refers to a delimited period, these two derivatives are based on the same principle. The buyer of the call option speculates that the price of the underlying asset will rise within a specified period or until the due date. This puts the trader in the position to buy the underlying at a meager price. The investor makes the actual profit if he immediately resells the underlying asset in a favorably stored case at a higher value. Thus, he can strike the difference of the market value at the beginning of the legal transaction from the value on the due date.

In contrast, the seller of the call option speculates on a falling price. At the same time, he assumes that the buyer of the right does not avail himself of the opportunity to acquire the underlying asset. Thus, the seller earns a profit with the premium and the further retention of the underlying.

Options and Warrants - A Comparison

Options are standardized products. These are traded as contracts on the futures exchange. By contrast, warrants are among the securities. They are issued by the issuers (for example, the banks). However, the issuer does not usually speculate on a falling price. The issuers issues another warrant, which should have a contrary effect.

Thus, the bank escapes the event of taking a risk as the price either falls or rises. The bank generates its profits from the commissions it receives for the issued warrants.

Warrant:

- is issued by an issuer who simultaneously sets the price
- the risk of insolvency borne by the dealer
- only long call or long put possible

Option:

- is provided by each market participant
- no risk, as the legal transactions are hedged
- the price is determined by the options exchange such as EUREX
- the conditions are standardized
- everything is possible such as long call, short call, long put, short put as well as combinations thereof

In principle, options and warrants are quite similar: both are forward transactions based on a previously established underlying asset. This value is also often called an underlying. For both variations, underlying of the following financial instruments may be available:

- Shares
- Currencies
- Indices
- Raw Materials
- Bonds
- Futures

Note: Options are highly transparent as their market value is published on the stock exchange every day. By contrast, warrants issued by the issuer have less transparency.

Trading Based on the Acquisition of Rights

The origin of these speculation products can be found in the Netherlands in the 17th century. At that time, the first tulips were bred there. Sometime after its introduction, the tulip became a popular flower in Holland. Eager flower growers set out to grow specific varieties that would bring in a lot of money. More and more interested flower lovers ordered the particular types from the florists, although they had not yet been brought to market. To give their action a firm reason, they paid for the tulips. In return, the florists offered to purchase a certain amount of tulip bulbs at a fixed price on a specific date. This created the basis for the first option.

In principle, the buyers did not want to invest their money at all, but their will was entirely directed to the exercise of the legal business. However, that could change if the tulips had lost significant value by the exercise date. In this case, the flower buyers were still obliged to purchase at the agreed price, and the tulip seller made a deal.

Note: The development of the option meant that the merchant had no choice during the time the options were created. He had to pick up the tulip bulbs at the previously agreed price, whether he wanted it or not. That could mean a huge win or bankruptcy for him.

The exercise right then and now

The development of the option lasted for a long time. In particular, the exercise obligation has changed over the years. In the early days, the buyer had to exercise his acquired right. If he had been authorized to buy 20 tulip bulbs at the price of 200 guilders, he could redeem them on the agreed date of purchase. If the tulips had risen in price, because the species and genus of this variety had suddenly gained in popularity, the dealer benefited from this advantage. He was then able to sell the tulip bulbs with a profit margin of one hundred percent.

If, however, the demand for this variety of tulips has declined in the meantime, then the tulip bulbs might have been only worth half the purchase date. Yet, even if they had not been worth anything, the businessman of the time had a duty to take off the tulips. The flower bulb buyer was not allowed to indicate that he wanted to renounce the trade. He had to pay the agreed amount of money to the florist and take worthless goods home. This circumstance has completely changed to this day. For the current options offered on the market, the investor can decide whether he wants to exercise his right to end the term or not. The investors enjoy these benefits today:

- if the financial product does not perform as desired, the highest possible loss is the risk of losing the option premium
- the default risk is therefore manageable since there is no commercial obligation
- Traders can still benefit from the better prices if they wish

Note: Financial products due to the transfer of a right now offer traders some advantages over other trading opportunities. If you find that your trade is different than you would like, you can now accept the loss of the option premium and let the transaction expire. You can calculate your risks in advance and act accordingly.

Advantages and disadvantages compared to warrants

Options have some advantages over warrants. This is especially true in terms of the risk involved. With both speculative instruments, traders with small capital can also trade through an account. The investor is not obliged to exercise. On the other hand, he can use the fact that the legal transaction has expired. Also, he has the opportunity to sell the financial derivative, in the American variant even before the maturity date.

Therefore, the investor does not necessarily have to have high financial reserves actually to invest in case of need. Options and warrants are tradable without having to buy the underlying asset. However, there is a unique feature in the warrants. These are rarely actually practiced. Its purpose serves above all the speculation on a profit advantage after a resale.

A lever can be used to multiply the profit of an option. However, it should also be noted that the risk of loss also increases if the price does not appreciate in the predicted way. In this case, traders can lose all their capital. The seller can always reap the option premium.

Both derivatives are used as a speculative instrument. On the other hand, they are an excellent way to hedge another position in the portfolio against loss. This is called *hedging.*

The development of the option

An option gives the investor the right to buy or sell a financial product at a predetermined price. He is not affected by the obligation to exercise the law. He can also forfeit it, losing his option premium at the same time. However, since this is his only investment, the risk of suffering a loss can be kept to a minimum. This benefits the calculability of the legal transaction. For these speculative instruments, the due date must be observed at a predetermined date. In the American variant, the product can be ordered at any time, which is only possible at the exercise period in the European form. Investors take less risk when buying or selling the right than when trading in warrants. In the case of warrants, the trader bears primarily the issuer risk, which is significant if the issuing bank suffers insolvency. Investors can disproportionately share in the performance of the underlying by investing in derivatives themselves by using little capital. In percentage terms, the option value reacts more strongly to changes in the price of a commodity than the value of the product itself. This effect is also called *leverage.* However, dealing with the presented derivatives is best recommended for experienced traders. There should be enough knowledge as well as some trading experience since trading on the stock exchange involves risks.

The Importance Of Your Mindset

It's easy to meet with people every day, who think differently from each other.

It is also easy to notice how, among the different mentalities of people, some patterns are evident. And with the word *'mentality'*, I mean the way of thinking or reacting to everyday events and perhaps, in due course, to those unexpected events.

It is said that every head is a world. That every thinking being on this planet perceives its surroundings differently. Well, what each of us sees as reality, is certainly nothing more than the representation of the universe, which our brain manages to make us understand. It's a matter of specific perception.

Now, if our brains interpret the variables of the universe, each in its way - to put it a certain way - then, why do we commonly find that people tend to follow massive patterns of behavior? And worse, ridiculous behavior patterns?

Why does it seem that the more individualistic and independent we preach to be, the more we tend to go in packs together with the other members of our species, towards the first ravine we see?

My criticism today goes against those who do not think for themselves, and instead, let others do it, following others irrationally or blindly.

«Thinking is one of the most difficult tasks of this life. That is why very few people do it. Who does not resolve to cultivate the habit of thinking, loses the greatest pleasure of life. » - Thomas Alva Edison

This is a call to take the reins of our lives, to realize that it is we who define our present and with it our future. To open our eyes to the stupidity that others have imposed on us whose ends are apparent.

Let's not let ourselves be manipulated; let's not let others be those who define our destiny, nor our direction. We don't have to accept that it is the others that move us like puppets. Why should we be the puppets?

There are lots of cases in society, however, and to get into detail, a typical example of this is employment.

What is the job? Employment is a necessary evil.

Approximately 95% of the people who work do not do it because they want, or because they like it. But because it is their turn. Why do they need money, and why their mind is not enough to give themselves a better life, far from orders, strict and absurd rules, and little time to devote to themselves and their loved ones.

Maybe it's all a matter of fear, or perhaps it's cowardice. Be that as it may, and from any point of view, it is absurd.

Why do we seem to have to live our whole lives doing what we don't want ? Because someone else told us that it should be like that. Because we were programmed to accept such inconveniences since we were little without saying a word. Because we fail to think and avail the enormous opportunities on offer all around us.

We are not robots, but sometimes, we look like it.

And regarding work. Just think about how many people have become rich working? ANY!!!

No, the rich - or those called financially free - are those who discover that the essence of life is not in money. You do not worry about money, but living being working for money, it is absurd. And that not making the necessary decisions to achieve effective maintenance is extremely risky.

Leaving my life in the hands of another, it seems risky, in fact.

The world is continually changing. Today, thanks to the new technologies, we have significant advantages at a general level for our lives. However, so much change is generating fear and indecision, so the advances are ahead of the backward.

The victims of change do not realize that life is NOT as before, that opportunities are changing and, therefore, the schemes under which we develop day by day. And, employment is no stranger to this situation.

In the industrial era, it was a great idea to study hard, graduate, get professional cardboard. Find a good job and take care of it until retirement, and then be old, live off the pension.

However, there are lots of disadvantages to it. And all mainly, because THE WORLD IS CHANGING. But more important than the world is changing, is that people don't realize it. This is critical, obviously.

SO SIMPLE.

Companies now cut staff every so often, do not want to pay pensions, because they involve exaggerated cost overruns (and more in times of "crisis") ... create modalities of contracts in which benefits are evaded and if that were not enough, time of these contracts, when perfect is one year.

The work is little and poorly paid for these days. It is said wisely that employment is slavery, spread over 8 hours a day.

You only get paid when you work, and if that were not enough, if you have a month of vacation a year, it is something exaggeratedly good.

You miss the good times with the family, and you miss raising and educating your children, you miss being with those good friends, ENJOY LIFE.

And so? If I don't work, what do I do to live? It is the question that people immediately throw at me, feeling confused with my premises.

And the answer to this is straightforward.

What did the creator of Coca-Cola do to live? Look for a job?

And Bill Gates, creator of Microsoft?

Robert Kiyosaki?

etc....

All those did something very different from 99% of people. THEY DREAMED WITH A DIFFERENT LIFE.

THEY EVIDENCED A CHANGE OF MENTALITY.

They dared to imagine that all this could be different and that indeed, seeing life from another approach, life could be better.

«Madness is doing the same things, expecting different results» - Albert Einstein.

Now more than ever, it is straightforward to undertake with all the comforts we have, information, communication... among others.

And I don't suggest leaving work right now and starting a business. But if I suggest making my own objective decisions, without prejudice to external interference, and giving high priority to the important, over the urgent.

All changes take time, and improving our quality of life will not happen overnight. However, to get from one city to another, at least I need to get in my car, and then start.

So ... why not start today with our path? Why not today, why not now?

Why not forget all those stupid prejudices that our society has injected into our minds by all means?

Why not have deaf ears before the crisis and other hoaxes?

For fear? Or maybe because of cowardice?

It is time to leave us with childish arguments and face our destiny. Face our problems and know exactly what we want for our lives. Take the right path, and fight to achieve our dreams.

How hard can it be?

Or rather... how difficult have they told you it is?

But... the same... some entrepreneurs still need SLAVES.

In your hands and head is there, choose the life you want.

Emotions vs. Facts and Strategies

The conflict between these two concepts is the key to the human psyche and the heart of our customers. But how and, more importantly, in what relationship should facts and emotions stand? Antoine de Saint-Exupéry gives us a famous clue: "If you want to build a ship, do not call the men to fetch wood, but teach them the yearning for the wide sea." The rest is easier.

Facts are naturally provable facts. Thus, to a certain extent, price, performance, and various other factors can be compared. So we are moving at this point on the rational level. For decision-making, whether consciously or unconsciously, many emotional criteria are added.

Studies conclude that 70% of buying decisions are made on the emotional level. Even the rational motivations, which account for only 30% of this decision-making, are not entirely free from psychological factors.

The reason is that we conclude transactions, daily necessities, or capital goods because the performance - even the illusion of it - is worth more than the monetary equivalent. The customer sometimes has to be brought to this realization first. To specifically address this fundamental emotional level, one aspect of marketing has become increasingly important for some time now: so-called *neuro-marketing.* This science has recognized that in marketing strategies, occupying emotion fields is more important than general design features of the performance offered. A purchase decision can, therefore, also be described as an *"emotional benefit assessment."*

The combination of picture and sound

The trick is now to extract the core message of service and then accurately transport it to the emotional center of the target group. With media in picture and sound, you can achieve the desired effect with professional advice and implementation, even on topics that are not emotionally tainted at first glance, such as spare parts for the industry. Which plant manager does not need reliability, high quality, reliability, and - as a result - after gaining their prestige? A skillful mix of media turns your need into a need, yours, and, hopefully, yours as well.

So far, I have not been able to determine a gender-specific discrepancy regarding emotional response. However, specific topics are more male or female. So a few months ago, I had a conversation with a good friend, who regularly travels in the areas of airplanes named by me as a show-off class because of above-average professional success. He was seriously concerned that his neighbor on the last trip was wearing a much more expensive watch than himself. The conversation ended with the remark that I would not be able to recapture the last 15 wasted minutes of my life.

Conversely, in a cosmetics shop, I involuntarily took care

of the amusement of my teenage daughter, because, following the advice of a trained shop assistant, her overpriced product would "make my beautiful eyes stand out even better ..." happy and with the purchase made, leave the action. How could that only happen to me...

Be More Productive Not Busier

I do not have the time. I am too busy. How often do you hear these two little sentences every day? Far too much, anyway. And honestly, you never achieve exceptional results when it is you who say them, these sentences. So stop being busy and be productive, to accomplish more things, get tangible results, and have the time to entertain yourself!

Perhaps you should make a list of things you absolutely must do today. And the important word of this sentence is *absolute*. The problem with this kind of list is that it never ends if you do not select what is essential - you can add tasks to the shovel and end up spending so much time building this list that we do not even do one. You will understand, this is not the right solution. You should never have to go over 8 points, and again, if you go over five, make sure it's essential. The list should not include things that everyone does (shopping, going to class), but specific points that bring you closer to your goal: read a chapter of a manual, establish a plan for your next presentation, etc.

Learn to do only one thing at a time: yes, being multi-tasking is a talent. But do not overdo it! When you think about it, multi-tasking is efficient when you know how to brush your teeth while you read the newspaper, it saves time.

On the other hand, for actions that require understanding and reflection, it is better to do one thing at a time. When you do something, do not do anything else at the same time. If you think of something else, write it down on a post-it and try not to think about it until the end of your activity. Then, you will resume the post-it and think about your ideas, but not while you focus on a specific action.

Finally, you can keep a productivity log. It seems like extra work, and it is, or at least it will be until you're used to it, and it's a handy tool. So what should you write in your journal? First, list your objectives: those of your life or only of your year, whatever, but you need long-term goals. Then, each morning, write down your list of things that need to be done. Tell them how it went: did you finish everything? How did you feel working? Was it a chore, or was it rather pleasant? Look for trends: times of the day when you feel more productive, the company of some people that can be beneficial or harmful. Finally, you will know exactly how you operate. And you will not need any more general advice because you will know exactly what you need to do or avoid. You will become quite good at *prioritizing*.

Set Your Goals

Peng! Set goals - and the rocket goes off! I used to be so naive when I defined the following formulation:

I was convinced that I had set a strong goal for myself or our company. It was just a vague declaration of intent.

At that time, I had done a lot of wrongs. Today, I know that the achievement of goals begins with the right objective. This foundation must be strong and clean. Otherwise, success may be nipped in the bud.

How to set your goals so that you have the best foundation for your success is outlined in this section of this chapter. Here I have put together five principles that I apply when I set a new goal.

1. Set your goal with the SMART formula

When I ask others if they have goals, I often hear spontaneously, "Of course, I have goals!". If I drill something, it often turns out that it is only vague wishful thinking - as in my previous example.

Maybe you already know the SMART formula. However, many people don't know anything about it; let alone define their goals.

That is fatal! Because precise goal formulation is just as important as the input of exact target coordinates in a navigation system.

The SMART formula is quite simple:

- Write (if possible only) a sentence in the present-day form with your very concrete, own goal formulation (Show specific).
- In this formula, you need a measure to check that you have reached your goal (M as measurable - e.g., not "a lot of money," but "100,000 €").
- The target should electrify and attract you (A how attractive).
- Also, the goal should indeed be high, but

reachable (R as realistic).

- Most importantly, you include a date in your goal formulation until when you will reach the goal (T as scheduled).

Check your goal formulation for the aspects mentioned above; then, you have an essential foundation to reach your goal.

2. Find a strong why when you set a goal for yourself

The more significant and more challenging your goal, the more critical it is that your motivation, your why for the goal, is crystal clear and strong. Especially under challenging phases and hurdles - which always exist - you need it. Otherwise, you fold in quickly and give up.

I have experienced it several times that I had set myself an "empty goal" with a weak *why*. One that I may have thought that I must "achieve" or was somewhat foreign and did not come from myself.

Think in detail and in peace about why you want to reach the goal. This inner power is critical! Make a note of everything that comes to your mind. I use my success journal.

Also, very important is that your goal is in line with your values. It makes sense, therefore, that you know your values exactly. Because the more your goal is carried by one of your values, the more intrinsic motivation you have.

If you want to get to the core of your motivation, it can help if you repeat the question of why several times by asking a new why question for your answer.

For example, you have set the goal:

"On 31.12.2019, I have saved € 50,000 on my time deposit account."

Why do I want to reach the goal?

"Because I want to fulfill the dream of a camper."

Why do I want to fulfill this dream?

"Because I need to be able to travel independently."

Why is it essential for me to travel independently?

"Because freedom and self-determination are my most important values."

By doing this, you can better understand your intrinsic motivation.

In this example, you could then unite motorhome and freedom in your why, which emotionally charges you much more.

3. Connect your goal with a visual anchor

Your subconscious mind is your most important ally for your success. Since it works through images and emotions, you should give it such signals so it can support you.

Therefore, we always create or seek a powerful visual

motive when setting a goal. It works as a great stimulant for the subconscious mind to support you.

If you have formulated a strong why for your goal, you may automatically feel an emotional inner image within you. Try to make it more visible.

It's not about the target visualization that should accompany you on the way to your destination, but rather about the "cover picture" of your target story. It should serve as a simple, memorable anchor that you always have ready to call, that keeps you pushing harder for your goal.

Be inspired and search the Internet or magazines for motives that resonate with your goal. Of course, you can also let it appear in your mind's eye. However, I like it when I can print a motive together with the goal formulation or save it on the phone or as a wallpaper. So I have it always present in mind.

4. Set goals with the right time horizon

I'm not a fan of target planning with daily, weekly, monthly, and yearly goals. So I do not think about what I want to achieve in a given time, but set a goal and think about when I can reach it.

These are usually the goals that I aim for in a period of two to six months - rarely even more. Of course, this can vary individually and from one goal to the next.

- When I set a goal, I first check it with the following two questions:
- Can I see what specific actions I can / must do today to reach my goal?

- Can I effectively sense the impact of these actions on my goal?

So I can tell if the size of the target fits, if the chosen period is right, and if I need to adjust something, for example, by breaking down the target again.

I tend to advise you on shorter goals. So you automatically get more "train on the chain." You see much more clearly what you have to do, see the effects more directly, and have to accelerate.

On the other hand, if your goal is still a long way off, you may be stuck with irrelevance forever, because "there is still so much time left." Then you may have to shout (too) for a long time, oppress yourself to extraordinary deeds and later forfeit.

5. Commit yourself to your goals

If you set yourself a new goal, you should nail yourself to it so that you can not quickly row back or give up.

I recommend three things:

- Consider a reward for the case of success.
- Make punishment for you if you can not do it.
- Tell others about your goal and the first two points.

You should celebrate success and reward yourself when you reach your goal! So think about how you'll reward yourself if you can do it. This is very important! You may also be able to use the mental image of the reward as a visual anchor. I do that often.

It's just as essential that you do not elude the punishment you set in the event of failure!

How hard you want to be, you have to decide for yourself. When defining a punishment, you should realize that you have to! Pull it through consistently. Otherwise, you'll lose your face in front of you! If you - as recommended - have initiated others, it will be much harder for you to seek escape.

Therefore, tell others about your destination, preferably several people. And also, what punishment you have considered in the event of failure. Ask these people to ask you about it regularly and to specifically discuss the target date if you have reached your goal.

Be aware that your success begins with the right purpose. In the past, I often did not achieve goals because I did not know the connections and therefore lacked this stable foundation.

The five principles described here will also help you to create the right base on which to achieve your goals.

Stay tuned! Your way is the goal!

More Sleep

It's six hours for Elon Musk, five to six for Richard Branson, and only four for Marissa Mayer at Yahoo times: The nights of tech entrepreneurs are short, sleep is almost nonexistent in the daily routines. Work rules of life.

The short night has become a figurehead for workaholics. Polyphasic sleep patterns describe a phenomenon in which people nod for a short section several times a day and forego the classic eight hours. The " Five-AM-Club " brings together people who want to start the working day as early as possible to get rid of essential things in the morning.

What the two phenomena promise: maximum productivity with little sleep or getting up early. You could say that fatigue has become socially acceptable. Because who is tired, he must have worked hard. Anyone who stays awake at night struggles with showing commitment to his job. However, anyone who goes to bed early or spends more than eight hours in bed is considered lethargic, sometimes even lazy. Sleep is overrated, of course.

The mystification of sleep deprivation is not explained. Anyone who studies scientific research realizes that sleep, as time-consuming as it may be, certainly makes sense. The body needs the time of rest; at night, energy is drawn for the new day. Lack of sleep has been shown to reduce attention spans, memory retention, and response time.

Sleep is important for performance

As early as 1996, researchers June Pilcher and John Huffcutt found out in a meta-study that sleep deprivation severely impairs the ability to function. For their study, the researchers evaluated the data of 1,932 people out of 143 study coefficients. Above all, the mood of a person suffers from permanently short nights - perhaps this explains the "terrible depths" and the "relentless stress" that Elon Musk described on Twitter in the middle of the year. The cognitive performance also decreases, even more than motor skills. Recent studies confirm the results.

Of course, such meta-studies can not reflect the individual requirements of the individual. Even though lack of sleep can cause problems, one night does not have to be eight hours for us to recover. What counts is the balance between sleep and wakefulness, also called *homeostasis*. In simple terms, we can only sleep if we are awake long enough. Usually, the optimal waking phase is 16 hours. It can also be shorter or longer, depending on the individual.

If we stay awake much longer, the sleep pressure increases. This is usually not a problem because we can go to bed earlier the next day. However, those who only go to bed at one o'clock in the morning and get up five hours later do not only experience short-term but also long-term adverse effects. In chronic sleep deprivation, overweight and diabetes threaten.

The Internal Clock - for whose research scientists were awarded the Nobel Prize for Medicine in December 2017 - also plays a role here. She determines if we'd instead get up early or be late. If it gets out of balance, it can cause problems. Anyone who has to get up early every day, even though he is a late-sleeper, suffers from a kind of chronic jet lag. This is what researcher Till Roenneberg found out in his *"Munich Chronotype Study 2006"*.

If we always rebel against our internal clock, perhaps because we want to belong to the Five-AM club, it can lead to illnesses. Shift workers have a higher risk of heart disease and cancer. Roenneberg has also found that people who do not follow their internal clock smoke more often - even if the correlation is not clear.

The perfect sleep rhythm does not exist

The big problem: there is no guideline for the internal clock. Everybody is ticking differently. An experiment from the 1960s proves this: In Andechser Bunker, subjects spent up to four weeks at a stretch - without sun, without watches. Researchers at the Max Planck Institute wanted to use this method to find out whether the daily routine is controlled by the sun or by the organism. The result: "All day-periodic processes observable under natural conditions are retained," wrote researcher Jürgen Aschoff in 1981. However, the processes shifted: The rhythm looked a little different for each subject; for many, it went beyond 24 hours. Historians assume that continuous sleep is not innate but a cultural product.

Perhaps it can also be explained by cultural conditions that tech companies boast of short nights. At a time when work not only means merit but also creates a deeper meaning for many, short nights have become a status symbol. The lack of bed rest seems to serve as a testimony to how much one uses for his cause: See how hard I toil, I even renounce to sleep for it!

Fortunately, there are always people who are embracing such trends. For example, Microsoft founder Bill Gates says he needs seven hours of sleep a night to be creative. Facebook CEO Mark Zuckerberg states that he has never been an early riser. In the early days of the social network, he is often not supposed to have entered the office before

10.30. And for Amazon boss, Jeff Bezos eight hours of sleep make a big difference. "I'm trying to make that a priority," he once told Thrive Global. "For me, that's the amount to energize me."

The Importance Of A Long-Term Vision

Let's talk about the influence of your perception of the world on your behavior and especially the "temporal" understanding of the world. Let me explain: most of the time, we are in *"short-term perception"* mode. When we decide to make a pizza to eat, we will say that we are in this mode of perception, we use our short-term vision. You can have an excellent reason to eat this pizza (it's okay, no time to prepare something else...) However, with a concept of the medium / long term, you would tend to limit consumption.

It's not a judgment, just an observation. If you become aware when you eat this pizza that in one hour, you will have a big hit, due to the drop in hypoglycemia that will cause its consumption (medium-term vision), that you eat a food that does not bring anything positive to your body and that it is likely to deteriorate in the long term (weight gain, increased risk of disease...) so this pizza will be immediately less attractive.

It often takes a violent shock for the man to realize that he is bullshitting (diseases, accidents, trauma...). It is usually after this first ring of alarm that he will pay particular attention to those little things that are important in the long-term. In this example, the food, since this is a field that can quickly be disabling (your physical and mental shape depends on it). Do not fall into the trap of ease at all costs, and it is often the best way to complicate things for the future.

Let's go back to the original subject. Here I took the example of food, but the principle can apply to many other areas.

If you are on this personal development, I certainly do not need to remind you how important it is to have at least a small idea of what you want to become in the medium and long term if you wish to achieve something essential or enjoy every experience of life thoroughly.

Here are some areas in which it seems to be interesting to apply the principle of long-term vision:

Your future: the importance of having values and setting goals. Also, understand that you can only progress step by step and that you need to establish a set of objectives to make each step a reality. Many men give up when they find that the path is long between the starting line and where they want to reach on arrival. Americans use an expression that seems perfectly suited to the "baby steps" situation. Like a baby who walks on all fours and who will eventually become an adult capable of running the Paris Marathon in 45 minutes. You have to know how to take time and not focus on instant results. Rome wasn't built in a day, after all!

Your diet: Socrates already said, "Let your food be your medicine and your medicine your food. "The junk food from time to time in front of a good football game or the last Sofia Coppola is excellent, but it is certainly not sustainable hygiene in the long run. The body is a machine that requires constant maintenance to function properly. The trap is to think you can eat, move, and reproduce its excesses of youth by believing that you will pass through the cracks. Think again, even the Mona Lisa is suffering the ravages of time, and you will not be the exception that confirms the rule. Take the lead and consider that this is also part of your personal development. Be Ready!!!

Your Seductive Ability: When you discover seduction sites and communities, you are always happy to swallow tons and tons of books on techniques/tips and tricks to chopper more. Again, this is the simplest, and it brings the most instant satisfaction. But it is a work on the bottom that will be the most exciting and rewarding in definitive. If we speak of "inner game," it is not a coincidence. It makes sense to dig deeper in this area than to get stuck on technical issues "and if she tells me that, and if she does that ...". This will allow you to make concrete progress in the long term, and the rest will quickly lose its importance.

You have understood the principle, be careful not to see either only in the long run. You have to know how to stay connected to the present and enjoy the small, immediate pleasures all the same; it's equally important!

Investor vs. Gambler

At very high risk, completely uncontrollable and unpredictable, yet more and more people are fascinated by the possibilities of winning the lottery, online casino,

211

scratch cards, video games. Does pure mania or gambling have any analogy with riskier and more profitable investments?

Similarities between gambling and investments.

The analogies clearly do not stop at the purest marketing: little difference, in substance, passes between the tissue and the footballer who promise you lavish gains by sitting at the virtual table of a Texas hold'em game and a banker who reassuringly promises the prodigious multiplication of your money by investing in bonds, small caps shares, etc.

In gambling, a certain sum is put into play and invested in one's fortune. Unlike what many claim, there is no real strategy to win and win over the various Superenalotto, roulette, scratch cards, slot machines. But as much luck is needed when embarking on a high-risk investment: potentially very profitable, but equally prone to the laws of Chaos. The axiom that " there is no 100% secure investment, and as risk decreases, earnings decrease " seems to confirm this initial impression.

The "virtual" dimension of various online casinos find logical parallelism in online trading platforms where a usable interface and the ability to see earnings and losses almost in real-time can lead to forms of compulsiveness and dependency. In the case of online trading, however, it is possible to somehow dampen the obsessive nature (which takes over, especially when you lose) through information, or expert advice.

Moreover, from a purely "human" point of view, the attitude of the gambler and the stock market player is characterized by the need, the desire, the need to feel the thrill of risk, adrenaline accentuated by feeling master of destiny, able to dominate the infinite variables of the law of chaos.

It is therefore essential to know how to identify, both in gambling and on the stock exchange, that value called *"Certain Equivalent,"* which in the case of gambling is relatively simple, in the case of equity investments is more complex and regulated by economic calculation rules defined.

The similarities between these forms of investment are therefore varied, but they mostly relate to more purely psychological and personal than technical factors. This is a vital point of the game.

CHAPTER 3

WHAT IS FOREX

Novice traders may have difficulty understanding how forex trading works and they often wonder if currency trading really works.

This chapter explains in detail the foreign exchange market, commonly known as FOREX.

What is Forex? Definition and Explanation

The forex (Foreign Exchange) is the foreign exchange market, where currency pairs like EURUSD or GBPUSD are traded. Forex is an over-the-counter (OTC) market where investors or speculators buy and sell currency pairs.

Forex is the currency market, and currencies, unlike most other tradable assets, are as economic instruments as economic indicators. If countries were companies, currencies would be their actions.

The basic terms of Forex Trading

Knowledge of the language of forex brokers will not make you a great trader, but it will help you understand the data and information needed to become one.

Here are the most important terms in forex trading:

- Currency pairs
- Forex Quote
- Pips

- The spread
- The margin
- Forex Financial Leverage
- The swap
- The lot or the size of the contract
- CFDs
- Forex platforms

Any investor who wishes to engage in currency trading must understand what *forex* is and the basic conditions of this market. Testing *forex* trading on a demo account is a way to learn and better understand forex.

Forex quotes

The currency pair is a crucial concept for the basis of forex trading. For example, the EUR / USD pair. The Euro is called the base currency. The US dollar is called the listed currency. The valuation of the base currency against the listed one gives us the forex quotation.

If we look at the EURUSD currency pairs or other currency pairs on the trading terminal, we see two digits, the bid and ask price. They look like this: EUR / USD 1.1234 / 1.1240. This quotation tells us that we can buy a euro with 1.1240 US dollars because it is the amount requested by the bank - the selling price.

At the same time, we can sell one euro for 1.1234 US dollars - the offer price. It is easy to see that, in general, a bank buys a currency at a lower rate and sells currency at a slightly higher cost. Banks can do this because they have more influence than brokers.

You cannot simply buy or sell EUR /USD, as you would, for example, with the shares of a company. This is because the currency pair EUR / USD does not exist. Money exists alone, not in pairs. Traders speculate on future price movements without buying currencies.

In forex, profit is realized by the appreciation or devaluation of one currency over another. Suppose you buy euros and sell US dollars (using the currency pair EUR / USD). To make a profit, it is necessary to sell US dollars once the Euro is valued against the Dollar.

There are two things to consider. First, traders never buy or sell physical currency. Secondly, buying and selling take place in all transactions.

Which currencies are traded on forex?

The discussion on how forex works would be incomplete without a review of the most popular activities available to a trader.

The most popular currency pairs in the world - the US dollar, the Euro, the Pound, the Japanese Yen, and the Swiss Franc - are part of a group of significant currency pairs called EURUSD, GBPUSD, USDJPY, and USDCHF.

There are three other conventional currencies in Forex trading: the New Zealand dollar, the Canadian dollar, and the Australian dollar. If they are associated with the US dollar, we get the group of minor currencies: NZDUSD, USDCAD, and AUDUSD.

All other currency pairs in forex trading are generally

referred to as "exotic currency pairs" and represent less than 10% of all foreign currency transactions.

Who works in forex?

The most important players in the forex market are:

- Central Banks
- The States
- Other Banks
- Cover Funds
- Investment Funds
- The Brokers
- Professional And Private Investors

Among the forex market participants, central banks have the most significant influence on the formation of exchange rates. A central bank is, in fact, the currency provider for the country in which it operates and is, therefore, the offer on that market. Their decisions have a very significant impact on the price of currency pairs.

Small investors, like retail traders, slightly influence the market, but this influence is visible only due to their large number.

To understand forex, it is important to know that the demand and supply of currencies are continually evolving and you can see the price trend on a tick chart on a trading platform, for example:

Understanding the Forex Market

In the economy, supply and demand design is a model that explains the formation of prices in a free and competitive market. The same principle applies to the foreign exchange market.

Every time you buy a currency, you create more demand in the market, which drives up the price. Similarly, whenever a currency is sold, a surplus of supply is created, which pushes the price of the currency down.

The impact of each purchase and sale on the forex market is directly proportional to the trading volume of each transaction.

The philosophy of price balance is the key to understanding how online currency trading works since all economic events in the world have an impact on the market.

Factors that influence FOREX

Several factors influence the forex market and currency prices:

- Interest rates
- Inflation
- Political, economic events, and natural disasters
- Economic growth rates
- The offer and demand of a currency pair

The online broker industry

The functioning of the currency market could be imagined as an ever-changing ocean. There are many fish in this ocean. From the largest to the smallest, depending on their purchasing power.

There are many important players, such as national banks, multinationals, hedge funds, etc.

There are also medium-sized fish - private investors, companies that need forex to protect themselves from currency risk, etc.

There are even smaller players - online brokers, smaller banks, and small investors.

Most of the above-market operators have direct access to the interbank foreign exchange market. They can do it, simply because they exceed a certain threshold of funds. This means that they can change currency directly without intermediaries.

The smallest player - the plankton of the financial ocean - which floats, trying to survive long enough to grow, is the currency trader, i.e., the individual investor.

The buying power of a trader is generally so insignificant compared to the big fish that he needs a forex broker or a bank that provides a trading account with financial leverage and real market access through a trading platform.

To understand forex, it is essential to know that there is no trading on its own as an individual without a forex broker that makes intermediation.

Forex trading is the activity of buying and selling currencies. Forex trading is carried out for speculative purposes or to hedge the exchange rate risk through a trading platform.

How Is It Analyzed?

The analysis is not only the key to success in trading, an analysis is, to a certain extent, trading itself. It's the only thing that makes currency trading work.

The two main methods of market analysis are *fundamental analysis* and *technical analysis.*

Fundamental analysis is an advanced form of financial audit, only at the national or sometimes global level. It is the oldest form of price forecasting that looks at an economy: the current phase of the cycle, relevant events, future forecasts, and the possible weighted impact on the market.

The fundamental analysis relates with national GDP and unemployment rates, interest rates and export amounts, war, elections, natural disasters, economic progress, etc. Fundamental analysis requires an understanding of the international economy, addresses factors that are not yet taken into account by the forex market, and works for long-term investments and exchanges.

The disadvantage of this type of analysis is the element of uncertainty created by many complex parameters.

Technical analysis is a younger form of market analysis that deals only with two variables: time and price. Both are strictly quantifiable, explained by the market, and are undeniable facts. This is why for many currency traders studying charts works better than doing fundamental analysis.

When drawing support and resistance lines, identifying key levels, applying technical indicators, or comparing candles - you discover what forex trading is without examining the causes of supply and demand.

To simplify, fundamental analysis is an economic detective with elements of future forecasts, while technical analysis is visual price-time archeology combined with statistics.

Winnings favor trained people

The lack of training is the reason why so many novice traders fail before they can even genuinely understand forex trading.

Some people, due to the nature of their business, present forex as a pseudo-scientific gambling attraction that is almost like playing a coin, an attraction that has a better methodology to a certain extent, is more fun, has more prestige and the opportunity to make money very quickly.

As a result of this marketing, newcomers with little or no training expect to make a fortune starting at $ 10, with just a few key clicks. They jump into the market full of hope, and the market hits them hard and empties their pockets. This is neither good nor bad - that's why the market exists. Every time someone closes with a profit, someone else has to close with a loss.

Forex trading is an investment activity available for any trader who has a computer and an internet connection.

Understanding the word *"Trading"* is simple: it is

about placing orders on the stock market. Negotiation means an exchange between different investors on the stock exchange, who exchange different financial products.

The word forex is a term that refers to the currency market, on which different investors exchange currencies and other financial assets.

Currency exchange is an everyday activity that takes place every day around the world. Governments do forex; banks do forex; even individuals do forex.

Trade takes place through computer networks among all the world's traders, electronically. The reason why forex is the most liquid market in the world is that it is the most accessible. As a result, the most difficult to manipulate.

How to trade Forex?

The logic of forex trading is simple. A trader buys a currency pair in the hope that its price will increase. The trader sells the currency pair when he thinks the pair will fall.

For example, the EUR is at 1.0895 today. The trader believes that the price of the Euro will increase in the next 24 hours. The merchant makes a purchase order. Tomorrow the Euro is at 1.090, and the trader closes his position with a profit of 5 points. The amount of the gain depends on the size of the trader's contract for this exchange order. The gain can be 50 cents or 50,000 euros, depending on the size of the order.

Looking at this currency investment process in detail, we

realize that investing in forex is a little more complicated than ordering.

CFD is a tool that has transformed the financial market into what it has become today. It is a financial instrument that allows you to invest a financial asset, such as currencies, up or down.

The forex trader does not hold the underlying asset, but only collects the difference between the entry price and the exit price of the position. This also allows us to speculate on the decline in currency prices.

After finding his forex broker, choosing his trading account, a trader installs his trading software and finances his account.

Multiple trading tools are now available to traders to start trading forex online. If the trader wants to trade a particular currency pair, such as EUR / USD, or a specific configuration of the market, such as the level of support or resistance, the trader must be prepared for a forex order!

The rush to invest is strongly discouraged, although this may be compatible with individual trading styles or forex market configurations.

Technical or fundamental analysis is crucial for online investments. We can start by analyzing the favorable market conditions for entering the position, the management of the money, the duration of the transaction, an estimate of the volatility for the period, the expected macroeconomic events and, above all, the exit times from a trading position on the forex market. All this reflection must be done before placing the stock market orders.

Once again, ANALYSIS IS THE KEY to forex trading! It is essential in the psychology of the trader and the evolution of the balance of the trading account. It is the equivalent of a business plan for an entrepreneur who wants to start a business. The ability to find, analyze, synthesize all this information is essential for forex trading! Mastering these aspects of trading is what makes the difference between success and failure in online trading.

Once the trading strategy is well defined, the order is made with a simple mouse click on the trader's software. Order is the least important part of foreign exchange trading.

What Are The Advantages Of Forex Trading?

You are in control! You decide where you want to live, when you want to work, and how much you want to work. The word "unemployment" no longer frightens you. And when you are asked what your job is, you answer: I sell and buy money.

The crisis is no longer a threat to you! Why? Because during financial crises, almost all assets follow the same pattern. This is the market trend. While the general public prefers bullish trends, forex traders do not care about market trends - they can operate profitably both upward and downward.

For example, in 2008. Your real estate is depreciated. Some currencies lose their value. All this while crude oil is rising from all-time highs.

If you are an online trader, you know the three golden rules of trading in times of crisis: selling currencies, storing real estate, and buying oil.

Remember: financial speculation is a freedom of the capitalist world.

In a highly capitalized environment, currency trading with CFDs is one of the activities available to proprietary traders against economic tsunamis, earthquakes, and wars. Provided that you know, of course, what you are doing—the most crucial factor for success, of course.

Why invest in forex?

The market is open almost 24 hours a day, five days a week.

Forex is the most liquid market in the world.

Brokerage commissions are lower than in other equity markets.

You can trade forex from home; you need to have a trading account with a forex broker.

Understanding Forex - Conclusion

If this chapter is your first step in learning the basics of forex, don't stop there. Be eager to learn much more, and you will definitely thrive!

To better understand how forex works, we recommend that you open a demo trading account and try it yourself.

CHAPTER 4

FOREX SCAM AND HOW TO RECOGNIZE AND PROTECT YOURSELF

Online trading scams are a reality, even in Europe, where the number of fraud victims in trading is impressive.

In this section, you will learn how to protect yourself from forex trading scams:

- How to choose a serious and reliable trading site?
- How to detect a trading scam?
- What are your options if a forex trading scam occurs?

It is said that the forex scam in online trading will exist as long as the forex market exists.

As the patterns evolve, forex scam sites try to extort your money. But is there a solution to this problem?

Since there will always be a fraud in trading, make sure you don't fall into the trap.

Commercial scammers tend to turn to novice traders, who are desperate for an income or who have not yet practiced enough, and hence the most vulnerable in the market.

The best antidote is knowledge. The best advice we can offer is to learn the fundamentals of the forex market and develop advanced techniques.

Once you have mastered the market, you will no longer be an easy target.

For this reason, we always recommend that you continue your education.

Sometimes, forex scams bear the creator's name, like the Ponzi scheme, developed by Charles Ponzi.

However, one thing is common: forex trading scams often use expressions such as "an investment opportunity that is too good to be true" as a tactic to attract attention and get your funds. Unrealistic promises are often a bait.

That's why when you have no trading experience, and a fraudulent trading site will try to exploit your optimism and your fears.

Nobody wants to lose their money, and this will be a strategy that forex scammers will use to make you an attractive offer that you won't be able to refuse.

Did you know that the forex market is the largest financial market in the world, with over 5 trillion euros traded every day? Not only does it allow central banks and companies to trade with each other, or tourists visiting new destinations, but it also will enable speculators to take advantage of a market that operates 24 hours a day, five days a week.

There has never been an easier time to enter the world forex market. With a single click of a mouse, you can trade on the direction of the Euro, the British Pound, the Japanese Yen, the US dollar, or even the Russian Ruble! There are hundreds of currency pairs to trade from, so you are free to find the ones that interest you the most.

However, while the financial gains of trading on the forex market seem lucrative, it is not considered easy. Having a reliable trading education, a properly funded trading account, and a comprehensive understanding of risk management techniques are essential. Unfortunately, many unscrupulous individuals will try to cheat beginners with forex trading scams.

Traders deceive themselves

Since forex trading carries an exceptionally high risk, losses are inevitable.

Some traders are almost always undercapitalized and subject to the problem of gambling addiction and improper use of leverage.

Any speculator who works without the necessary skills plays effectively against the entire market as a whole, which has almost infinite capital, so it will almost certainly lose its initial investment.

Under-capitalized traders who have no information advantage should understand the different reasons why they think they can beat the market in such a challenging trading environment.

In any case, much of the total number of claims for fraud presented to brokers occur as a result of a low level of training in trading and market awareness, rather than for genuine scams fore.

It is always easier to blame others as a first choice than to take responsibility for our shortcomings.

If bad traders spent adequate time developing a consolidated trading plan and looking for the right broker rather than complaining about a predictable failure, they could become successful traders much faster.

Most good traders should be able to use almost all trading platforms with any broker and see very few differences in their results - it's that simple.

Once you accept your losses, trade with a studied system, and control the market, it will be much more difficult to fall into a forex scam.

Some Examples To Better Understand

But let's see now what the real cases of forex scam are and how they differ.

1. The scam on the trading site

Although there are, of course, many regulated and reliable brokers, many online trading platforms are scams. Before working with a platform, check its reputation and make sure it is not in the blacklist of your local regulation.

Trading with a safe and reliable tool is fundamental for having a productive and satisfying trading experience.

2. Scam Forex Trading

Although the forex market is a risky market where money can be lost, it cannot be said to be intrinsically a scam market.

When we talk about forex trading scams, we're talking about scams perpetrated by fraudulent trading platforms.

If you practice forex trading with a severe and regulated broker, you will receive adequate training and practice on a demo account, reducing risks to a minimum. It's highly advisable to practice on a demo account first.

3. Scam forex high-frequency trading

High-frequency trading is the high-speed execution of financial transactions using algorithms.

This is an automatic trading category that raises ethical and regulatory issues but is not illegal.

4. Forex scam with robots

Not all trading robots are the same. Trading robots are not a scam in themselves, but many trading sites have made the sale of trading robots a fraud.

This is because they promise their victims, novice traders of course, quick and easy profits.

5. Forex scam with social trading

The social trading, trading or copy, is to replicate the experienced trader's operations.

Although this is a new practice, the risk of loss is not inferior to that of traditional trading.

6. Forex scam with false repayment

The reimbursement fraud is a double sanction imposed on

the victims who have already been scammed the first time.

It consists of making believe the possibility of recovering all or part of the funds lost by a fraudulent broker, in exchange for a sum of money, to fall back into the same scam.

These entities are typically bogus banks, fake law firms, or various debt collection companies.

7. Forex phone scam

The regulated entities we usually work with have obtained our data legally. Furthermore, with the GDPR (General Data Protection Regulations), it is possible that we must give our permission to send commercial offers.

But if an entity that we do not know contacts us to offer us an investment, we must be extremely cautious because it is probably a forex scam.

Clues to Identifying a Forex Scam

If we pay attention to the following indicators and signs of a possible forex scam, we will have many more opportunities to avoid it, so keep reading carefully!

1. Trading and training systems without evidence

There are many scammers selling trading systems and training programs.

When you ask them to provide proof of their business history, they avoid the answer.

There are also many traders offering their systems without

any service. These traders offer "infallible" trading systems but have no valid proof of their trade history.

Therefore, the best option is usually to access free training programs from regulated and reliable sites.

2. Spam Mail Requiring Personal Information

Scammers can also ask you for personal information, for example, by e-mail:

- Your full name
- Your phone number
- Your address

Don't give your contact details to someone you don't completely trust.

Beware of brokers who do not present a risk warning on their web page and in their marketing material.

Even if they do, read the warnings carefully because the scam is in the details.

Remember → Your data could be disclosed massively and instantaneously.

3. Watch out for great promises

Easy money-making? No way! Don't believe someone who tells you it's easy to make money with a monthly rate of return of 20%. It does not make sense.

Forex and CFD trading takes a long time to be a profitable option.

There is no easy money here. If you invest the time needed to practice and learn to trade correctly, you would have a great source of income. But with work, effort, and above all, with time!

4. Unprecedented

Never work with someone who refuses to give you the necessary information. Whether it's a broker, a trader, a trainer, or a fund manager.

You should always do a quick online check to see if the person or company is legitimate.

As Mr. John Naisbitt once said: "We drown in information, but we lack knowledge."

5. False stories reported by the media

A prevalent form of forex scam is viral news. For example, the story of a child who became famous during the night.

According to New York Magazine, a young man from Queens earned tens of millions of euros thanks to the stock actions he was negotiating during lunch hours at Stuyvesant High School.

What happened was that he never really made those profits, since all his earnings were made on a demo trading account.

How to deal with a forex scam?

Have you been a victim of a forex scam? There are two types of resources, depending on whether or not the company that created you is regulated:

- If the entity is controlled, you can contact the Financial Ombudsman Service or the Financial Services Compensation Scheme (FSCS) if you believe this company has cheated you. This can be done by e-mail or by filling out a form.
- If the institution is not regulated, it is possible to apply to the ordinary courts of the place where the fraud occurred.

Please note that these procedures are free and wary of any entity that promises to release funds lost in exchange for a fee or different registration fees.

We have noticed that there are victims of double fraud with false reimbursements, and therefore, it is advisable to check these sites to find out if the institution in question is authorized to operate.

How to choose a suitable broker

Although trading and scams go hand in hand, fortunately, it is possible to trade without risk in a severe trading site.

To do this, it is necessary to verify two crucial points:

1. Check on the FCA website that your broker is not blacklisted for illegal financial sites.
2. Search for opinions and evaluations online on the broker, as well as correctly read all the information on financial security on the broker's site. The difference between a legitimate and an illegitimate is obvious!

When making these checks, pay particular attention to the spelling of the broker's name: illegal sites often use a name similar to that of a severe and regulated broker, changing only a few letters: it's identity theft.

Identify a forex scam

So, if there is trading, is there a scam? Not necessarily.

There are several regulated and reliable brokers, whose reliability can be verified on the website of the financial regulatory entities.

Trading certainly involves risks, but it is a severe and legal activity whose image is unfortunately obscured by the forex scams carried out by some criminals.

To make sure you don't become a victim of a scam, always use the services of a regulated broker that has positive opinions online and is 100% transparent in its compliance policies.

The fascination with quick and easy money will always be present, so the most important thing to do is to understand what is needed to succeed in forex trading. And for this, the best way is to try a free and risk-free demo account.

CHAPTER 5

RISK & MONEY MANAGEMENT

The profitability of investment must always be related to the risk of capital loss that it makes you take. Above all, this risk must be in line with your investor profile.

For your wealth, good risk management is essential.

Investment solutions that are both profitable and risk-free do not exist. All investment proposals in this direction must be avoided at all costs because the real "risk-free" rate of return is traditionally given by the OAT 10 years of France. And that is currently negative.

Some investments offer a capital guarantee at any time. This is the case, for example, of the Livret A, which reports, net of social security contributions and taxes, 0.75% per year. This is also the case of funds in euros of a life insurance policy, which distributed an average of 1.8% in 2018; however, it takes correct social contributions (17.2%) and the taxation upon withdrawal.

Calculated risk

This attractive remuneration compared to the current level of bond yields, is linked to the better return on investments made in the past. That is why the erosion of euro money yields is slow.

Beyond these levels of expectation of remuneration, any investment necessarily entails a greater or lesser risk of capital loss.

This does not mean that you should avoid taking systematic risks with your investments. The risk must be calculated and match your investor profile because a reasonable risk, in the long run, is paying for your wealth.

The 80-20 strategy

For savvy investors who have time to spare (at least eight years), a strategy known as 80-20 may be relevant.

It consists of placing 80% of their savings on secure assets such as funds in euro life insurance contracts rewarded by Le Revenu and 20% on unsecured products, rather oriented in shares.

Thus, in the long term, the remuneration of the secured party will make up for any loss of value of the risky part. In the long run, your capital is more or less protected, even if the financial markets turn around. And if the markets are on the rise, the overall performance of your assets will be very attractive.

Investors with a more dynamic management profile may increase their share of unsecured assets. The ideal being always to diversify the underlying (equities, real estate, bonds...), maturities, and geographical areas.

Psychological factors often influence investment choices. Investors are thus characterized as overly optimistic when financial markets are expensive and too pessimistic when they have fallen sharply in these conditions, difficult to perform.

Invest regularly

To limit this, multiply the "entry points" to smooth the risk and avoid buying at the highest. For that, continually invest (every month, for example) on several supports to constitute you an average cost price.

Many life insurance policies also offer tailored management options that take the form of automatic arbitrage. Other equally exciting options limit the loss in the event of a decline in the financial markets.

By combining several of these options between them, you frame your investments and your maximum risk-taking — the guarantee of a serene investment.

CHAPTER 6

FOREX STRATEGY
Why use the Forex strategy?

Perhaps you, too, have heard of the fact that in forex trading, many people lose money. Well, we are certainly not here to deny the evidence, and we want to inform you as honestly as possible; the reality is there for all to see and offers staggering numbers regarding the winning and losing financial operators in the field of forex trading. In recent years, mainly, an unexpected massacre has occurred: about 90% of those who trade in Forex end up losing their capital over a period of time that can vary from 6 months to a year. Only 10% of financial operators succeed in bringing satisfactory results home, in simple terms, to earn well and consistently over time.

But at this point, a question arises: how is it possible that there are such negative statistics on online trading? What is this almost catastrophic fact that seems to leave no hope for those who approach financial products for the first time? From the analyses carried out by the experts, a tendency is clear: in recent years, there has been a boom in memberships in online trading, a real race towards the riches of the financial markets that does not seem to want to stop at anything, but the newcomers are ready to make investments in forex? It just doesn't seem like it, and the most meaningful explanation lies in the fact that you don't use a forex strategy. Let's discover together why using a forex strategy is a guarantee of success, but also the reasons why you can do it too... and immediately!

Free Forex Strategies: Find Them Here!

The forex is made on a scale; there are those who go down, and there are those who go up...

The trivial paraphrase of a famous saying we have given above can help you understand how things are going in trading. The fact that most retail traders lose does not mean that there is no one who scales forex, which means positive prospects for your trading account in terms of profits and profits, which would be unthinkable with any other online activity, but let's try to understand why there are many traders who lose and few who earn.

First of all, it must be pointed out that this boom, known from online trading, has led many people to start trading without any preparation. We are talking about people who are attracted by the earnings prospects that probably, having arrived at online trading thanks to some deceptive advertising, have used their capital as if they were at the racecourse to place a bet on horses. Fortunately, online trading on forex is something else or something that has nothing to do with a bet or any recreational activity.

Investing in the forex market is a severe opportunity that must be exploited professionally through the implementation of STRATEGIES. This is a word that sums up different meanings:

Forex strategy is not tactical: a strategy is a method studied in detail that has been developed to achieve precise objectives along a long-lasting path. A tactic instead is only a technique that is adopted to obtain a result in the short-term that often is not based on particular criteria, so here is that the tactic is similar to a bet.

Investment Plan: strategy in forex also means having a precise investment plan, all based on the capital you have available. The plan must contain monthly and annual objectives, the balance of income and expenses, and the planning of the daily investment activity, including a study on financial assets.

Forex Money Management Strategy: managing investment capital is an aspect of primary importance when doing forex trading. Too many beginners underestimate this aspect, and not by chance do ALL pay the consequences. The investments must, therefore, be weighted and well thought out, and the money must be rationalized for each open position on the market.

Forex "Technical" Strategies: in the last analysis, we must mention that for strategies we also mean the "technical" ones, i.e., those based on the use of technical indicators that are used to study the trend of financial assets on the short and medium-term, which are fundamental for intraday and multiday trading.

The Secret Advantage Of A Strategic Approach To Forex

As you understood from the previous paragraphs, choosing to approach the forex strategically allows you to obtain significant benefits and satisfactory results, but we want to close the discussion on the importance of strategies revealing a small secret that 90% of retail traders who lose money every day ignore or choose to ignore. Learning strategies can take some time and a certain amount of patience, but managing forex trading strategically offers you a little-known advantage that turns out to be decisive: a forex strategy like the ones you have the chance to know here guarantees you the average success in 75% of market positions for two reasons:

These are the same strategies that are used by experts in the sector with the only difference that here they are understandably explained to you without leaving room for empty technicalities that are ultimately only counterproductive and prevent bright and lasting learning over time.

The strategies are all based on the most essential and proven technical and fundamental analysis tools for financial markets. Even the use and understanding of these technical tools will be unaffected because our explanations are geared towards newcomers to the sector; on the other hand, an expert certainly does not need to contact us.

In the field of trading, there is so much misinformation and wrong information that we have decided to make the maximum clarity here by offering free forex strategies for all beginners who are looking for severe earnings methods. If you are not willing to learn and apply strategies with commitment, then forex trading is probably not for you, but if you want to get serious here, you find all the material you need.

Forex Intraday Strategies

In forex trading, there are no rules regarding the duration of the investments, that is the time span along which an open position is maintained. Every trader is free to choose his style without any conditioning, but it is clear that the general tendency is to do daily trading.

Intraday trading has great appeal, which is why among the forex strategies we offer here, intraday strategies have plenty of space and high effectiveness to allow you to make profits daily. But let's go into detail and see what the main types of trading are along with their relative advantages.

Medium And Long-Term Trading

When an open market position remains such for a period exceeding 24 hours, then one can speak of trading in the medium / long term. Many traders prefer this type of investment because it guarantees good margins of success, but for the most part, they are financial operators that have already been tested and experienced, able to cope with sudden changes compared to long-term forecasts and to management positions even for a few months to get dizzying gains.

Trading in the medium and long term is suitable for investors capable of making fundamental macroeconomic analysis. This type of analysis has a very mild impact also on the intraday and concise term forex, but we define fundamental analysis:

With the help of fundamental analysis, traders try to bring out the so-called "substantial value" of the financial product or asset, that is, its intrinsic value. This is a feasible operation for any asset, for the stock, as well as for currency pairs in the forex market and commodities.

The fundamental analysis lends itself, in short, to any category of assets on which it is possible to invest in forex or with CFDs.

To better understand what we are talking about, you can simply think of the stock market where, precisely, the shares relating to listed companies are exchanged, the role of fundamental analysis is thus easily identifiable: a structural analysis makes it possible to identify the strength of a company on the market (therefore the value of its shares) going to check what the deficit is and what the profits, and in general, what is the state of health of the company.

More specifically, the task of fundamental analysis is also that of understanding which external and internal factors can influence the value of that company, raw material, or currency. Once comprehended what are the factors that influence the assets, it is straightforward for the traders to understand which information to look for to place prudent and profitable investments based on the excellent information obtained.

Short And Concise Term

Intraday trading or day trading on Forex is undoubtedly the preferred type for all retail traders in the world, and the technique is to open and close positions within a day so that they never stay open for over 24 hours. It is a pleasant and exciting type of investment able to bring to life the sensations of the true trader, but above all to bring daily profits that are directly tangible to the trader, this perhaps explains the success of this type of trading and consequently also of the strategies of Intraday Forex. The intraday trading is much easier to manage than long-term; this makes it suitable even for those traders who do not have a very long experience in the field of Forex. Here is a compendium of features required of a trader to make intraday earnings:

- Stress management skills.
- Knowledge of investment assets.
- Technical analysis of financial markets on charts.
- Knowledge of short-term investment strategies.

Technical Analysis For Intraday Forex Strategies

Analysts call " technical analysis " the study which aims to analyze the price trend of the various financial assets in specific time frames, to understand how to participate in the market in the immediate future. This definition is in itself very fascinating because it reflects reality; technical analysis is a method of analyzing price trends that allows us to know the price trend in the short and medium-term with excellent approximation.

Being able to make a precise and consistent technical analysis means earning in most of the positions that are open to the market. Of course, you can't think that with technical analysis, you automatically earn. Still, without the technical analysis, the assumptions of the investment in the short and very short-term would disappear, and there would be no winning intraday Forex strategy.

Traders from all over the world analyze the market on

mathematical and statistical models. Based on technical/graphical indicators, which are widespread, financial operators obtain signals of entry and exit from the market that are always "fresh" and effective in most cases. The data and signals obtained from the price chart analysis tools are useful to understand when to open and close positions in the market and therefore help you save money and maximize profits. TECHNICAL ANALYSIS is ultimately the key to success in investing in Forex.

Forex Scalping Strategies: Fast Trading

If, as we imagine, you are interested in intraday trading, here you can find all the strategies you want, all studied and proven as they are used every day to earn from countless traders even among the most experienced. But if you are a lover of Forex intraday trading, you may also be interested in Scalping, the fastest form of trading there is. If you are looking for Forex scalping strategies here, you can find bread for your teeth; in fact, there are plenty of trading techniques suitable for those who want to act aggressively on the market to attack profit!

CHAPTER 7

STOCK TRADING

Stock trading is one of the highest yielding investments. The fact that many do not dare to bargain on shares is partly due to the lack of information about stock trading. We want to close these information gaps with the following share advisor. Because stock trading requires a knowledge base: we are going to show you what you need to consider when trading stocks and how you can achieve a good return even in low-interest phases.

What are public companies and shares?

The legal basis for shares and stock corporations can be found in the 410 sections of the Stock Corporation Act (AktG). A corporation (AG) divides its share capital into shares. The shares are sold to investors on the stock exchange. Each buyer thus owns a share in the issuing company, which receives financing support through the sale of shares. As a shareholder, shareholders also have a say in important company decisions. Investors exercise this right to participate in the Annual General Meeting. Any shareholder can either participate or instruct a representative to exercise their voting rights.

How do I make profits with stocks?

Shareholders benefit from the dividend paid and from the difference between the buying price and the selling price. A dividend is an amount that the corporation distributes to shareholders as a partial profit. Each share consists of two parts: the so-called *coat* and the *coupon*. The coupon represents the dividend entitlement that most types of shares have. The amount of the dividend will be decided in the Annual General Meeting and depends on the business results of the past year. If a fiscal year does not go well, the payout can be meager, or the company pays no dividends. While the dividend is usually paid once a year, investors can always make a profit by buying and selling stocks.

To achieve price gains

Shares are traded on the stock market. For this purpose, the trading systems of the stock exchanges continuously create selling prices and purchase prices for each share. If an investor buys a paper at a low price and sells it at a higher price sometime later, his profit is in the difference between the buying price and the selling price. This difference is also referred to as the *spread*. However, there are fees for each transaction and taxes on profits that reduce returns. The order fees depend on the custodian account, so it makes sense to perform a detailed custody account comparison before investing in securities trading and to find the custody account that suits your investment type and your requirements.

What do I have to pay for stocks?

At the first issue, i.e., the first issue of shares, the stock corporation and the bank accompanying the IPO determine the price of the shares. After that, the price is decided on the stock market by the principle of supply and demand. The information is either in Euro per piece or as a percentage and is independent of the nominal value of the papers. The sale price for shares is also called the *asking price*, while the bid price is known as the *bid price*. The stock exchange ensures that a fair price is given when trading stocks. The stock exchange receives commissions for the placement work.

Different types of shares

The Stock Corporation Act allows companies to issue various types of shares, as the issuance of shares is also called Initial public offering (IPO). The most important types of shares include:

- No-par value share: represents a share of the capital stock
- Par value share: has a fixed par value
- Ordinary share: is provided with all rights for shareholders
- Preference share: gives the shareholder preferential rights, for example, a higher dividend
- Registered share: belongs to a buyer known to the stock corporation
- Bearer share: belongs to an anonymous owner

The type of share does not influence price performance. Whether the stock price of a stock rises or falls, is subject to its own rules, which are sometimes difficult even for experts to see through.

Which factors determine the share price?

A stock exchange is a free market. This means that the

price depends mainly on supply and demand. The more investors want to buy a particular stock, the higher the cost of the private capital. If there are more sellers than buyers, the price falls. But why, at some times, are there particularly many investors who are interested in a particular stock, and why do several shareholders simultaneously sell the same security?

Price fluctuations: why do share prices rise and fall?

More significant price fluctuations are often observed during AGMs, so when public companies present their annual results. Even though it is known that a company has received a large order, this news has a positive impact on price development. By contrast, financial scandals or legal proceedings against a well-known company cause the prices to fall as the value of the company decreases.

The art of a successful stock trader is to find the optimal time to buy a paper at a low price and profit from the subsequent price appreciation. Since buying a stock is a long-term investment, shoppers should not wait too long for the right price. Even though a higher price is paid for a stock, over the years, the issue often recovers from other profits and dividends paid.

Unlike cash deposits on a savings account or a savings account, no regular interest is paid on shares. Nevertheless, equities are in a *well-stocked portfolio*, as investors call their portfolio. The purchase of shares is one of the long-term investment forms. Some shareholders retain their holdings for decades in the custody account. However, they must be aware that the share price is constantly changing, and the value of the securities may fall below the purchase price. If you sell your shares too fast when the price falls, you can suffer losses that can be avoided with sufficient patience. It's quite tricky.

Stocks as a pension

The purchase of shares is not suitable for a short-term investment. Dividends are usually distributed only once a year. Therefore, shares should be kept in the custody account, at least until the next dividend payment. Many investors buy shares for retirement or for long-term goals, such as educating children or purchase property as a retirement home. Equity funds, which invest many investors' money on the stock market, are also an alternative for acquiring individual stocks.

Shares or equity funds?

In addition to buying individual shares, numerous banks also offer equity funds and exchange-traded funds (ETFs). An equity fund collects the money of many investors and invests its inequities by the fund's guidelines. Many funds focus on individual sectors, conservative investments, companies from specific regions or countries, or securities with high potential returns. The fund shares are often offered from an investment of 25 euros, so this form of investment is also suitable for small investors. However, the return is not as high as buying individual stocks. This is because there are costs for managing the fund and the salary of the fund manager. To cover the expenses, the funds charge a sales charge, which the buyer has to pay.

ETF as an alternative

An alternative to traditional equity funds is an exchange-traded fund, abbreviated ETF. This fund is passively managed, so there are no high fees for a fund manager. Also, ETFs typically index. This results in a good diversification, as the diversification of the investment in different securities is called. Due to the diversified investment, losses of some papers are offset by the profits of other shares. Many ETFs show regular price increases. ETFs are often recommended for beginners who are currently entering the stock market because of lower fees and the high chance of a positive, high return.

Conditions for Trading in Equities

Beginners in stock trading must first acquire some knowledge about the process. To this end, serious advisers should be read, and the tips of well-known investors such as André Kostolany or Warren Buffet be respected. In addition to initial knowledge of the investment market, an investor must also have a custody account with a matching clearing account at his or her home bank or another bank. The purchased shares are kept in the custody account, from where they can also be resold.

Deposit account and clearing account

Many banks and savings banks offer a deposit account, often referred to as a deposit. The depot is not intended for daily payments. All securities held by an investor are recorded in the custody account. Accountants also need a clearing account to book transactions related to securities trading. This is either the checking account of the bank customer or, in some providers, even a money market account. Some banks offer free deposits, while other banks have custody account fees.

Deposit costs: Pay attention to the fees

Online banks, in particular, have free deposits in their offer, and also the billing account will not be charged any account management fees. Nevertheless, stock trading is not free. For every purchase and sale, there are order fees, which are different for each provider. Also, it may lead to the calculation of stock exchange fees and brokerage commissions. The amount of the fees investors know in the price-performance directory of the custodial bank. Also, the individual costs during the checkout are displayed.

As costs reduce returns, stock traders should compare the fees of different providers. The selection should also be paid attention to whether the bank has a free demo account on offer.

Free Demo Account

Some banks offer a free demo account that allows beginners to learn about stock trading. Account-holders will receive a virtual balance to buy any shares. The selected papers are not traded, but trading is only simulated. The price of the notional shares is adjusted to the current price fluctuations and changes regularly. The demo account allows beginners to learn different types of orders without risk and to try out investment strategies. For some providers, the offer of the free demo account is limited in time, while it is permanently available at other banks. A demo account is a perfect way to get to know the trade and understand the process for all those who enter the securities trading business.

Acting - online or in-person?

Stock traders who are well versed in stock exchange trading and do not need advice can independently trade through an online depository. After opening the account, the investor receives the access data for his custody account, including a clearing account. The order entry is online. Purchases and sales are executed immediately and posted to the accounts. As a rule, the providers of an online deposit require the lowest fees. Trading is possible on weekdays between 8:00 am and 10:00 pm for most online banks.

If you have questions about certain stocks or to buy, many banks offer orders by phone. Here answers either a voice computer or a consultant is directly on the phone. The calls are usually accepted only during bank opening hours. Besides, the fees for the telephone order acceptance are higher than in online trading.

If a trader maintains a custody account with a branch bank, he can also make an appointment with a trained securities advisor. The adviser provides comprehensive information on stock trading and issues an advisory report. Beginners will learn about the opportunities and risks of stock trading. Deposits at a branch bank, however, are usually more expensive due to the higher personnel costs, so it should be considered in advance whether personal contact with a bank account is essential or whether one can do without it.

Which stocks are suitable for beginners?

The 30 largest stock corporations are summarized in the Stock Index, abbreviated *DAX*. These include well-known names such as Adidas, BMW, Deutsche Bank, ThyssenKrupp, or Volkswagen. The DAX-listed brands are also known as *blue chips*. These are companies with a particularly high value. There are also blue-chip companies worldwide whose shares are listed in, for example, the American Dow Jones Index or the Japanese stock index Nikkei 225.

Beginners should first look at these stocks to minimize the risk of loss. As a rule, equities do not fluctuate too much. Therefore, investors can focus on other aspects of stock trading, such as the different order types. Often, the so-called index funds (ETFs) are recommended for beginners, as they are more cost-effective due to the automatic management and also have a high degree of diversification, which is why the price fluctuations are less.

How much money do I invest in stocks?

The most crucial tip when investing in stocks is that only money that is not needed in the short-term should be invested. Stock trading is a long-term investment. Therefore, the savings on the new car or vacation are not suitable for buying stocks.

Many investors choose to invest around 30% of their savings inequities. More important than the exact percentage of total assets, however, is a successful investment strategy that the investor should develop and stick to.

Under no circumstances should a loan be taken for trading in equities and other securities, as the risk of loss would lead to even more significant financial consequences. Invest only the money that you own and that you can forego in the longer term to get a high return.

Different Investment Strategies

One of the key tips from seasoned traders is that every investor should choose their investment strategy. This strategy should be maintained, even if stock prices are going in the wrong direction. To observe the development, the courses should be reviewed regularly. This does not have to be done daily. At least once a week, however, every investor should inform himself about the development of his portfolio.

Here is a list of the best-known investment strategies in stock trading:

- **Dividend strategy:** purchase of shares with high dividend payments.
- **Dividend growth strategy:** buy stocks with the highest dividends.
- **Momentum strategy:** buying stocks whose price has risen in the past and will continue to rise.

- **Reversal strategy:** buying stocks whose price has fallen and will increase again in the future.
- **Value strategy:** buying stocks below their value.
- **Index strategy:** Purchase of Exchange Traded Funds (ETF) that replicate an index.

Successful investors often combine multiple strategies to achieve the best return on trading stocks. The experts emphasize that an investor who trades in shares must also bear losses. This is also one of the biggest rookie mistakes: many inexperienced investors sell their holdings directly after the adverse price action has taken place. However, in such a situation, which is not uncommon, it is essential to keep a cool head and wait, rather than immediately resell.

Tips for Starting in Stock Trading

Every newcomer in stock trading must pay apprenticeship money and accept losses. But there are some tips on how to avoid typical rookie mistakes:

- *Patience pays off*

Patience is one of the most important virtues in stock trading. Price losses must not lead to panic sales but must be sustained. The savers should also note that every transaction is associated with costs. The fees for purchases and sales reduce the return and can even lead to a negative result.

• *Track-specific investment goals*

An investment in shares is not suitable for a quick profit. Successful investors have long been involved in the financial market and have also gained experience through short-selling. Therefore, an investor should not be too greedy but consistently pursue his investment objective. This includes critically questioning stories about supposedly quick profits of other stock traders and not following every trend.

• *Be informed about the stock market*

Newcomers to stock trading should familiarize themselves with the financial market and learn about some public companies. Experts advise dividing the fixed assets into different shares. Beginners should concentrate on fewer than ten stocks. Thus, the observation of the depot does not become too time-consuming. Also, the investor can react quickly to current economic news and market movements.

Investing in stocks is not suitable for every investor. However, anyone who acquires some knowledge about the stock market can make good profits with stock trading. Investors should invest money that they do not need urgently enough. Moreover, general interest in the financial market and patience are among the most important qualities of a successful trader. To make the first step towards successful securities trading, the book provides you with advanced topics such as the stock market, custody accounts, bonds, funds, ETFs, and leverage products sound information because knowledge is also the key to success in the financial world!

CHAPTER 8

SIMPLE STRATEGIES TO USE
Why use stock market strategies?

Here is a good question. Why is it worth using stock market strategies? You need to know that the financial instruments you are trading on, such as CFDs (contracts for difference), are already designed to be simplified and accessible for investment.

Even the platforms where you will find yourself performing from a practical point of view, your trading operations are very intuitive and can, therefore, be exploited both by industry experts who demand the possibility of trading professionally, via beginners who may never have put to this kind of tools but still want to create a monthly income by investing in the stock market.

One of the right reasons why it is worth learning the stock market strategies lies in the fact that we are sure that you too have always dreamed of finding a job that would not force you to move for long stretches, perhaps remaining stuck in traffic and city chaos, a job that does not oblige you to say yes to the boss on duty who may not even deserve to occupy that place, a job where you should not be forced to work overtime to be able to reach the end of the month charging you with stress and fatigue.

This is why we believe that trading with stock market strategies is the best possible alternative, not only offline but also online. Being independent in this promising world guarantees you the possibility to shake off the problems linked to the crisis to earn your freedom, even before the money, to become the master of your own life.

A thousand good reasons to trade with the right strategy

If you find yourself somehow, you have heard about the possibility of trading on the stock exchange, and maybe you know there is no way to do it online. If you want to take this path, we ask you not to feel intimidated or frightened by your possible future as a financial operator.

The stock exchange trading online has become a beginner or beginner's measure that it is. If, until today, you have only played lowly professions and do not have a higher degree, perhaps you think that you are not up to this kind of activity.

Perhaps you believe that the Stock Exchange and Markets, as well as the strategies to earn money, are beyond your means! Enough of this loser mentality.

The truth is that you are second to none, and you have the potential to be on a par with others and, why not, also to excel, especially in a world where meritocracy reigns like that of the stock market and financial markets on the internet.

Millions of people around the world have chosen the path of investment of their online capital, albeit very small. Now you can do it yourself by putting into practice the stock market strategies that we will propose to you during this guide.

Apply the right bag techniques

Do you think that all these people know every single nation and all the secrets of the financial markets to be able to earn a salary at the end of the month in this kind of activity?

This is not the case. Anyone who makes money from online trading does so from little to useful knowledge. It is, therefore, not a question of quantity; it is only a question of quality.

Few but good stock market strategies will allow you to become an established and successful trader who can afford to buy whatever he wants, in total independence, and without having to ask anyone for anything.

It is necessary to know as well as to apply the right bag technique. Learn it first through theory, then put it into practice in the field of trading, testing it continuously and optimizing it based on your trading methodology.

Do not miss the topics to come and immediately discover the best stock exchange strategies, the path that will lead you to become a real trader may be extended and tortuous, but in the end it will be worth it, and you will finally feel satisfied in an occupation free from conditioning and the harassment of the world of work as it has always known it.

If you start trading today, your old life will already be in the past, because you're about to be immersed in a virtuous circle of real opportunities to become an ace of stock trading. Cheers!

Difference Between Tactics And Stock Market Strategies

Modern stock exchange strategies have been devised to permanently change the old canons of traditional investment that made everything too slow and stiff, too challenging to apply, and this caused traders many problems and dissatisfactions, so much that many were eventually led to abandon this promising activity.

With the new strategies, the goal has been to make trading affordable and feasible for everyone, the doors are wide open, and anyone who wants it today can enter without suffering the typical problems of the past.

What it takes to make the most of the strategies that we propose to you in all respects is only basic knowledge of the subject of trading. Consequently, you are not called to know everything to start earning.

Therefore, trading does not mean having a degree in economics. After all, those who would be prepared today to face 5 years of studies to earn money, it is really too much time and too much sacrifice to put in place, so the techniques that you have to use to earn are simple but effective strategies that guarantee the success of the trades in most cases.

But because in stock trading, we talk about strategies and not tactics and because the former is much more successful and secure than the latter. The speech is very simple, and we want to clarify it with the following short definitions:

Investment Strategies

The strategy is the description of a long-term action plan used to set and subsequently coordinate all the actions that serve to achieve a particular, specific purpose. Strategies can be applied in all fields to reach the goal.

They, therefore, carry out the task of obtaining greater security by making a series of separate operations that help to reach an end goal. In the case of trading, we are talking about profit, which is undoubtedly the only primary aim that drives people to enter this business.

The simple tactic, on the other hand, is a course of action adopted according to the achievement of specific objectives, but in this case, we speak of small achievements in the short-term.

Adopting tactics would not be effective or satisfactory in the field of trading because it is not a structured plan, but simple plans to achieve small temporary objectives. In short, with a tactic you can also win a battle, but not war; winning a war requires a broader STRATEGY.

What all traders aim to achieve is a constant and lasting success over time that gives total security of a monthly income and specific collections on an annual basis. In stock exchange trading, it is possible to achieve all this by using strategies. Without strategies, you might perish as a trader very soon.

Applying stock exchange strategies requires attention and many precautions, especially at the beginning, when you are not much of an expert. In certain situations, when the markets become uncertain or careless, you do not know how to act, and you risk making mistakes.

At specific errors, however, the strategies cannot be remedied; in those cases, it will be the experience to act as a master and to suggest the right moves to make.

How much do you earn if you use the best strategy to invest?

With financial instruments available today, profit margins are simply impressive; operating in the right way, you can earn a lot of money even on a daily basis, but at that point, you have to take into account other factors such as the skill of the trader, the ability to avoid the losses, the amount of capital you have available, but also the small strokes of luck that from time to time can help to increase profits.

The amount of money that can be earned then also depends, above all, on the financial product you intend to use. There are not very marked differences but still tangible, depending on whether you prefer to trade forex, CFD, or investing in social trading.

Stock Market Strategies And Money Management

If you intend to trade on the stock exchange, there is no doubt that you will, sooner or later, have to come into contact with the rules of money management or all that concerns the management of money and your precious investment capital.

Money Management shows you the way to correct

money management, so it is fundamental in trading, but its rules are also applied in other fields that are as varied as in the domestic or business economy. Ultimately, the rules it dictates are quite simple and due to pure and simple common sense, but in any case, it will be necessary to observe them religiously to avoid running into severe problems in your career as a trader.

The creators of the first money management techniques had a clear idea that it was necessary to produce a new awareness of the use of money in their investments, for the first time imposing the concept of diversification and differentiation of the investment portfolio to reduce the risks of trading and losses on investment capital drastically.

A strategic approach to stock exchange trading cannot, therefore, ignore the knowledge of the fundamental precepts of money management that require you to always establish the spending limit and the budget available at the beginning.

In the field of trading, this will mean establishing the risks that you are willing to run within certain limits that not even an "Indiana Jones" of trading could ever think of crossing; otherwise, it would face economic suicide at the speed of light! The principles of money management help you put both the risks and the potential profits on the scales to understand if a particular movement on the markets should be exploited or not; in other words, it helps you to know if the game is worth the candle.

If you learn to put the rules of money management into practice, your long-term success can be practically assured, but even the short and medium-term will be more probable and easily accessible. In short, all this talk turns to a need for investment efficiency.

The best traders are those who can minimize losses, which not even the guru of the economy could ever avoid, and increase profits more and more.

The key to all this is precisely the fact that before learning to earn aspiring traders, the importance of learning to lose should be taught! Suffering losses and spilling money is a natural thing in trading, and you have to try to understand it and not give too much weight when a loss occurs.

The main rule of money management states that you should never, never, ever put at risk more than 5% of the total capital available in single trading operation.

Doing so would be stupid because it means that in case of loss, you should lose a lot of time trying to recover the negative position if you succeed. Furthermore, it is necessary to avoid losing more than 30% of the total capital available in a single trading day.

You simply have to recognize that when a bad day happens, you have to have the courage to turn off the computer or the device that you used to use to go for a nice walk and not run any further risk because it is clear that that day or you are not able to operate correctly or things in some way always row against you. It is the case to abandon the current session as soon as possible.

Best Strategies For Investing

In the following list, we present the best stock market strategies that you can use to succeed as a trader in the financial markets. Let's talk about very effective trading techniques to exploit with.

• *Adx Strategy*

The first strategy to which we want to introduce you is that which is based on the Adx, a very special but at the same time, easy to read trading indicator. This indicator has a rather intriguing history because initially, it was used for analysis only on the raw materials market, and later on, its inventor, Welles Wilder, decided to test it also on other markets immediately realizing its incredible potential.

If the markets are based on trend analysis, the ADX is the right indicator to find them and measure their strength. This strategy will be very suitable to find the best trends and exploit them to your advantage, increasing profits and always having the pulse of the situation under control.

• *The Cage Strategy*

This instead is a somewhat atypical stock exchange strategy and different from the others but equally valid and also very special to use and implement. Both beginners and professionals adopt it for its simplicity. The elements you need to make the most of the strategy are few.

CHAPTER 9

THE PARAMETERS TO CONSIDER

Operators use technical analysis to help them better understand what is happening in the market and gain a potential perspective of what can happen next. Many operators, who are new to technical analysis, often have misconceptions about what it is and what it is not and what you can do for them. There are five essential aspects of technical analysis that can, if better understood, help traders better determine entry and exit points, as well as offer clues about the possible future direction of the price.

1. All information is discounted in the price.

Fundamental analysts focus on things like earnings and sales figures to determine the appropriate "value" for a given stock. A technical analyst is less interested in "why" an action or asset is traded at a specific price, and more interested in "where" it can go next. In essence, a technical analyst believes that all the good and bad "news" related to the market or assets are already reflected in the price information.

2. The volume can offer important information.

Many price movements, such as breaking to a new high, for example, are generally considered of greater importance if they are accompanied by a higher than average volume of operations. For most technical analysts, the higher the trading volume, the more "valid" the break is typically considered since a large volume means great conviction and enthusiasm from operators. This is why the volume appears in the chart of all technical operators before any other indicator or tool.

3. Markets are driven by psychological factors, in addition to the fundamental ones.

The demand for a given value increases or decreases depending on the collective assessment that all traders perform concerning the real or perceived value of that value. For example, an announcement about strong sales and profit growth for a given company can make traders have a more favorable opinion regarding the shares of that company. As a result, the company's stock demand may increase. A technical analyst will try to identify this by recognizing the improvement in the price action and the increase in the volume of operations.

4. Prices tend to move in trends and patterns.

Public perceptions can change quickly. Sometimes, these changes affect perceptions about the stock market in general, or broader financial markets in general. Other times, these changes affect only a particular segment of the market or a specific stock. However, most of the time, the price of many assets moves actively without any concomitant "news" that can explain "why" this movement is occurring. This often makes it appear that price movements are random. However, experience has shown that price action often falls into patterns and "trends."

A "trend" can be defined as the general direction of a given price for a given time. It is assumed that a trend will be in effect until a clear signal is given that that particular trend has been reversed.

Types of trends:

There are three different types of trends: bullish, bearish, and lateral.

• *Bull Trend*

An upward trend is defined as a series of higher lows and higher highs over a given period of time. Connecting these rising lows with a trend line is a standard technical analysis tool that can help identify whether an uptrend is intact or not.

• *Downward Trend*

A downtrend is defined as a series of lower highs and lows. Connecting these high decreasing points with a trend line is a standard technical analysis tool that can help identify whether a downtrend is intact or not.

• *Lateral trend*

A lateral tendency is a series of ups and downs within a relatively flat or compressed range. Connecting these high and low points with a couple of trend lines can help identify the trading range. A standard tool of many technical analysts is to look for breakdowns above or below a defined trading range to indicate when a new uptrend or downtrend can begin.

The Timeframe Of The Trend

The time frame of the trend can play a vital role for many traders. Price trends can last days, weeks, months, years, or just a few minutes. It is essential to consider which period of time is the most important for your negotiation style. The longer a given trend persists, the higher it's meaning. In general, it is believed that the longer the period of time, the stronger and more useful the signals that are generated. For an intraday analysis, the trend with 1-minute bar graphs may be significant. For virtually all analysis time frames, minute-by-minute price changes are not substantial. The duration of the trend is divided into three-time frames:

- **Primary Trend**
  - This category includes trends that last from six months to several years.
- **Secondary Or Intermediate Trend.**
  - This category generally includes trends that last from one to six months.
- **Minor Or Short-Term Trend.**
  - This trend category usually lasts from one day to a couple of weeks.

Remember: "The trend is your friend."

Because the concepts of trends are so fundamental to technical analysis, many traders have a saying about "the trend is their friend." This adage suggests that operators take advantage of the primary prevailing trend, rather than operating against, or "fighting" that.

5. Work to increase your weight of evidence, not to find the Holy Grail

Trading signals can provide operators with a clear set of criteria to search and help them better identify possible opportunities. However, using only a technical analysis tool or an indicator only gives you a fraction of the image of what is happening with the market or the asset. On the other hand, the use of too many indicators can result in an operator feeling overwhelmed or having "analysis paralysis" because of the number and, sometimes, the exchange signals, in conflict.

Many operators look for signs of a combination of only a few tools and indicators to build their "weight of evidence" to help them make more objective and less emotional decisions instead of reacting to any price movement in a reactionary manner.

No technical tool or indicator will have a perfect signal register. There will always be the possibility of false or conflicting signals. Nor is there a specific number or combination of tools or indicators that work for everyone. That is why it is essential to identify some clear trading signals that you understand and that best adapt to the trading strategy.

What's Next

It is an excellent idea to examine more closely the technical analysis tools that are of interest to you. Doing this can help you better understand how each tool works, so you can determine the best way to adapt to your trading strategy and plan.

CHAPTER 10

START WITH THE SIMULATOR

Investing in the stock market, as the experts point out, requires substantial knowledge and experience to control the risk and make the appropriate decisions at the right time. That is why a *virtual stock market simulator* can become a fundamental tool to start trading with securities eliminating the dangers one can't afford much with one's hard-earned capital.

These simulators generally offer very advanced interfaces, a virtual economic fund to invest, and real-time information. That is to say; they have all the tools and functions necessary to learn how to invest in an online stock market as if we were in the stock market itself.

Many of these computer programs belong to banks and brokers specialized in the stock market or markets such as Forex (such as Plus500). These applications, from our point of view, are more complete than the simple stock market games that we have found in the market for decades or than the apps that have overwhelmingly increased in recent years.

In this chapter, we are going to analyze five exciting simulators for beginners, so that you can get valuable experience in a virtual stock exchange system before giving way to the real world. Most offer free demo accounts, although in some cases, we can find companies that request a small payment in exchange for using their platform. A small expense that is worth taking on, and that can save us many dislikes in the future.

Why Use A Bag Simulator?

Investing in the stock market is not especially difficult, but it is essential to have good knowledge to avoid greater evils. If you want to achieve high profitability, you have to take risks, but doing it blindly can be a real disaster for our pocket. It can be suicidal, financially speaking.

That is why it is essential to train previously in everything related to the markets and their operation. For this, you can go to the editorial fund of the National Commission of the Stock Market or the Madrid Stock Exchange, where we can find practical guides and handy tips for beginners and more advanced investors.

Having the advice of an expert is also a guarantee, but if you prefer to take the road alone, we recommend that you settle the bases well before playing with real money. The risk, as we have repeated, is high if it is operated without the necessary knowledge. The stock market is not a lottery that can make you rich by investing a few euros, so you should know all the mechanisms of the market entirely to understand *where* and *when* to put your money.

In this learning process, a good stock market simulator plays an essential role. With these tools, you can play with fictitious money, see how your decisions affect your income statement, and, most importantly, create solid pillars to leap to the real world of investments.

Another advantage is that the companies that offer these

simulators allow you to directly operate with real money from the same or similar platform, so you will already be familiar with the interface. In many cases, it is only necessary to convert your demo account into a real account and make an income, without changing the program.

Pay for a bag simulator?

Many people are wondering what the best free bag simulator for beginners is. It is true that in the market, we can find compelling tools that do not require the payment of any amount, but it is also true that skimping on this section can be a real mistake.

Creating a CFD bag simulator that offers guarantees entails a considerable programming expense and high operating costs. That is why some companies ask for a small subscription in exchange for their use that does not usually reach 10 euros per month. A minimum amount for a tool that tells you how to learn to invest in the stock market from home and that allows you to practice with all the guarantees; it's worth it by any standards, of course.

Also, it is widespread that with that small fee, the user has access to manuals, tutorials, webinars, and other teaching materials to support the practical part with theoretical foundations. Investing in the stock market in the short term is not recommended, so all this material can be of high relevance to fix concepts.

The Best Bag Simulators

Once this preamble has been completed, we will analyze

five of the most exciting simulators in the market. All are backed by companies with ample experience in the sector (they are banks or brokers) and are well above in quality and performance of simple stock games (we do not recommend using these games as part of your training). This listing is sorted alphabetically.

• *Active Trade*

This real-time stock market simulator offers users an account with 100,000 virtual euros so they can practice without fear of losing their money. It has personalized support and, most importantly, with courses and trading programs taught by professional traders.

With this tool, you can create your strategy, control your investments, find the companies that best fit your profile, and get detailed information on more than 18,400 shares. Essential functions to create your profile as an investor and locate those opportunities that you can take advantage of in the real world.

• *IG Spain*

The demo account of this stock market simulator allows you to invest in an online stock market in a risk-free environment. This free account has a virtual fund of 20,000 euros and offers graphics and prices in real-time. Also, you can check from your mobile or tablet to continue operating anywhere, even if you don't have a computer. The interface can be customized to suit your tastes and your style.

This demo account, however, does not offer all the

276

functionality of the real platform. The most notable differences are the following:

- Transactions made through the demo account are not subject to slippage, interest or dividend adjustments, or price movements out of the negotiation.
- Transactions can be rejected if you do not have enough funds to open them, but they will not be denied due to size or price issues.
- The graphics packages have no cost.
- The positions will not be closed if you do not have enough funds to cover the margin or current losses, something that does happen in a real account.

• *Orey iTrade*

Another easy-to-use bag simulator is that of Orey iTrade. With this tool, you will learn to invest in both the Spanish selective, that is, in the IBEX 35, as in other critical global exchanges. All online and free, since you can try it without cost and obligation.

Through its interface, you can access stock quotes in real-time and different analyses, comparative, and graphical tools. The account begins with a virtual fund of 100,000 euros to start investing.

• *Société Générale*

This trading simulator seems to us one of the most interesting since it will allow you to delve into the world of warrants, something that is not available in most of the free tools. The simulator of this French bank makes available to its users 10,000 fictitious euros to negotiate on the listed products of Société Générale and test their investment strategy without risk.

To start operating, you must register on the website www.sgbolsa.es. Registration is free. Also, the entity usually raffles gifts such as mobile phones or tablets among its new users, one more argument to try the Market Simulator, as they call it.

To use the system, follow these steps:

- Register on the website www.Warrants.com.
- Connect to the website www.Warrants.com or the simulator using the e-mail and the registration password.
- Access the simulator from the Tools menu of the website www.Warrants.com.

• **Tradertwit**

The Tradertwit simulator catches our attention since it has enormous educational value. It is not free (although it is cheap), but instead offers training and a compelling platform. They have a lot of news from the sector, an exciting collaborative platform, and thousands of interactive analyses.

We like what they call *"the challenge."* It is something like a 50-level training program that puts users in challenges to move from level to level. In each of them, you have to follow instructions, such as the maximum lever that can be used or the maximum loss streak. There are also objectives to be achieved.

Based on these criteria, the user can carry out operations of buying and selling currencies, indices, or raw materials — an excellent way to learn while having fun and competing against other users in the community. Also, the best usually takes real prizes.

CHAPTER 11

THE MOST COMMON QUESTIONS ABOUT TRADING

1. Can you live on trading?

Yes, just as you can live from medicine, from being a teacher, from being an architect, engineer, or lawyer. You require the same weapons: education, training, practice, guidance, discipline, perseverance, and a lot of determination to be a great professional in your field. Trading is no different. Perhaps many people have been wrong to think that when opening an account in a broker, funding their accounts, and starting trading means having the results to live from trading in less than what a rooster sings and being millionaires. Very wrong!!! It's like pretending to be a surgeon overnight. If you can live from trading, the question is, do you have what it takes to do it and achieve it?

2. What do I do to start trading?

The first and most important thing is to educate yourself about what trading is and how to do it effectively. Start by knowing the nature of trading, what it is about, how you win, who participates, how is the market that has been chosen, etc., are some of the things you should keep in mind. Don't get to war empty-handed. Go prepared. How? Find someone to inspire you, to teach these things, to guide you, invest money and time in your education. There are many online trading schools, and you can be overwhelmed at first by searching, but choose the one that has a simple system, that its philosophy resonates with you, and that has your feet set on the ground. Avoid those that promote phrases like "fast millionaire trading in the Stock Exchange," "trading is straightforward," etc. You have to be realistic, and a school that tells you from the beginning what is trading, how it works, how it is earned, how it is lost and that it is not as easy as many want to make it believe in profiting, is a school that is worth considering.

3. When will I start seeing results?

When you have firmly rooted in a simple trading system, faithfully and disciplined, fulfilling your trading plan and adequately managing the risk-benefit, paradoxically, you will also begin to see the results when you detach yourself from the results and focus on the process. The process of trading involves the observation and reflection of our performance, the emotions experienced, the most frequent mistakes and annihilation, the analysis of the logbook, and the correction of the things that you can change and improve. You will begin to see results when, in addition to all these things, you continue working on your mind without giving up.

4. How much money can I start trading, and what broker should I use?

It depends on each broker and the instrument you use. If you want to trade stock options in Thinkorswim, for example, you will need at least $ 2,000 to access the options. If you're going to trade with stocks, you will need

$ 25,000. With the other brokers, it will be different. On the website of the brokers are the most frequent questions and customer service that can take you from all doubts regarding minimum money to start, documents such as funds and how to remove, etc. Find the broker that is regulated, that has a good reputation, that other people are using and tell you about their experience.

5. How much money per month can I generate by trading?

The one that allows you the size of your account and the amount you are going to invest per operation, as long as you have the capabilities required to make money consistently. This brings us to question # 1. It's that easy.

6. How to achieve consistency?

Consistency is achieved by having consistent behaviors and actions. That is, if I have planned trading that tells me what it looks like an opportunity, where to go, where to place the stop, how to manage and how to manage risk, and do it over and over again which tells me that plan consistently then I'll have consistent results. But if you change the policy, each has a stop or every time you have a losing streak then you will go into an endless loop in which as emotional and impatient trader will modify or change it again and again, the plan and the results will be different. This is what happens to 95% who lose money doing trading; there is no clear, defined, and precise plan to follow consistently, disciplined, and with a lot of confidence.

7. What is the best strategy or trading system?

The one that is simple to understand, that you can even explain it to a child and the child understands it. Stay away from those systems that require more than five different indicators, that your attention away from price action scribbles filling your screen and does not have proper management of risk-benefit. The best strategy or system is simple, clear, proven (functional), and above all, fits your personality and type of trader. The method of a trader may not be the system that suits you; for that reason, you must define what type of trader you are if you are scalper, intraday or swing, and of course, your risk tolerance (conservative or risky). These are just a few things to consider when choosing a trading system.

8. I have lost much of my capital; what do I do?

If you have lost a large part of your capital, it is because you do not have a clear, defined and proven trading plan, there are no consistent behaviors that lead to consistent results; emotions dominate you, and there is also no proper risk-benefit management. In that sentence is the answer to this question. What you should do is simple: make a clear trading plan with a clear and straightforward strategy, try it in a demo, manage risk-benefit properly, trust 100% in your plan, work on your emotions being aware of them before, during and after of operations, record, and evaluate to be able to learn from your failures.

If the results are positive, return to real account and repeat the process focusing your attention on the emotions you experience and your reactions.

9. What actions do you recommend operating to start?

I recommend trading stocks that do not have a widespread, that are not very volatile and offer economic contracts near ITM. These are terms that you may not understand if you are starting. Once you know what the ideal requirements are, go to the Finviz map of actions and look for the best-known actions in each sector, write them down, go to your platform and look at their contract and spread grid, so you are choosing and removing from the list until have your ideal portfolio of at least 6 shares.

10. I have no time to trading regularly, what are my options?

You can choose to do swing trading. The swing will allow you to open an operation today and close it several days later. You will need a trading system that suits this style, have your stop defined so that it protects your capital while you are away, and periodically review operations. Some brokers have mobile applications that allow you to monitor operations from your cell phone. If the situation is that you cannot trade in the morning, you can choose to make a trading plan for the afternoon hours, and it will work the same.

CONCLUSION:

The fear of losing in online trading

Among the most severe and frequent psychological risks that a trader can run, there is undoubtedly one of ending up crushed by the dangers of "loss aversion." That is, the fear of losing could excessively limit the trader's ability to act, leading him to bring him back into a condition of extreme prudence that could throw off any strategic plan.

It is known that traders who fear losses are much more likely to maintain their losing positions, for example, than traders who can accept short-term losses and move on to more profitable transactions. Maintaining the positions at a loss, without respecting your strategy plan, is a serious mistake, as it jeopardizes the stability of your portfolio, not only by accumulating negative results but also, and above all, by preventing capital from being profitably used for better operations.

But how to know if you are afraid of losses? If you want to see if you have any tendency to lose to aversion or not, ask yourself if you have ever been inside a losing trade beyond the point where you knew you would have to go out. Behavior that you may have held because you hoped that the financial instrument on which you have bet would have reversed its course from unfavorable to positive, eliminating the losses accrued.

If the answer is definite, you must immediately become aware of the fact that you are "victims" of an excessive aversion to losses. Therefore, you must become aware of these characteristics and directly ask yourself how to overcome loss aversion quickly and effectively!

Well, in this sense, the best way to overcome a loss aversion prejudice is to operate with stop-loss orders set at the opening of the position and managed automatically by your broker. Many traders claim to have the habit of operating with a "mental" stop-loss, that is, with a stop loss level at which they think and promise to act if the financial instrument touches that level. However, too often, traders fail to act on their mental stop losses. So they let their emotions get in the way and start to rationalize their choice to stay in the trade until they think it will turn their direction upside down.

Conversely, as soon as you enter a position, set your stop-loss order with the broker, in such a way as to wipe out the emotions at this juncture.

Excessive Self-Confidence

Forex traders have to compete not only with other traders in the forex market but also with themselves. Often, as a Forex trader, you will be your worst enemy yourself! On the other hand, as human beings, we are naturally emotional. Our ego wants to be validated - we want to prove to ourselves that we know what we are doing, and we can take care of ourselves. And we also have a natural survival instinct!

All of these emotions and instincts can be combined to provide us with particularly essential successes. However, most of the time, our emotions will prevail and lead to losses, unless we learn to control them.

Many Forex traders believe it would be ideal if you could completely separate yourself from your emotions. Unfortunately, this is almost impossible. Moreover, it must be remembered that some of your emotions will help you improve your trading success. The best thing you can do for yourself is to learn to understand yourself and pay attention to specific elements. For example, do you know how to manage excessive self-confidence?

Overconfidence is exaggerated esteem in their Forex trader capacity. If you find yourself thinking of yourself as someone who has understood everything, who has nothing more to learn... then you are probably suffering from an *excess* of trust and confidence in yourself—not conducive at all!

Traders who are too self-confident tend to get in trouble by trading too often or placing significant transactions, trying to cash out as much as possible. Inevitably, an over-confident trader will end up trading unwisely and unreasonably, risking too much on the only operation that goes wrong and quickly running out of his account.

The best way to overcome the prejudice of excessive trust is to establish a rigorous set of risk-management rules. These rules should at least cover how many positions you should open and manage at one time, how much of your account you are willing to risk on a single transaction, and how much of your account you are ready to lose before taking a break from trading and re-evaluating your strategy.

Be The Master Of Your Own Life

Happy Trading